MID-LIFE CAREER RESCUE: WHAT MAKES YOU HAPPY

HOW TO CONFIDENTLY LEAVE A JOB YOU HATE AND START LIVING A LIFE YOU LOVE, BEFORE IT'S TOO LATE

CASSANDRA GAISFORD

PRAISE FOR MID-LIFE CAREER RESCUE SERIES

"More and more people today, either through choice or necessity, are looking for new and more fulfilling ways of working and earning their livings. Old ways are breaking down. Today, sacrificing your deeper passions for the security of a paycheque is no guarantee of security. Following your heart and deeper self is the new security. In this book, Cassandra helps you find your work, inspiring you to consider new possibilities, gently guiding you beyond limiting thinking, and helping you find your own true self and authentic work."

~ Nick Williams, Author of The Work We Were Born to Do: Find the Work You Love, Love the Work You Do

"Stop. Don't leave your job and start a business until you've read this book. I was pleased to see Cassandra tackle the real challenges starting a business poses. Things like finding the right business, how to start with little or no money, and how to leverage it to create a great lifestyle, to name a few. If you get to a stage in your life where you want to leave your job and start a business, this book will help you. Each chapter focuses on one highly practical aspect of starting your own business."

~ Barry Watson, Author of #1 best-seller Relationship Rehab

"This book has given me another kick up the bum, to write it all down, work from the end result backward, envisage the 'as if' and build the staircase I need to climb."

~ Cate Walker, 5-Star Review

"Makes you think and offers strategies to make it work! I met Cassandra about 17 years ago after being made redundant—the advice she gave me and the challenges she threw at me even then have remained in my psyche and continue to give me motivation. So reading her books it's easy to hear her voice, continuing on with that motivation. I usually skip reading other people's stories as many of them don't translate to real life for me. But many in this book resonated, in particular, the opportunity that I have to follow not just one passion, but I can follow all three, and make them work! With ageism alive and well, I've had so many rejections for job opportunities that it's a matter of survival that you have to tread your own path—find opportunities for yourself. This book has given me the confidence that I CAN make it work."

~ L.A. Brown, 5-Star Review

The tiny, brilliantly colourful hummingbird
symbolises the messages in this book.

This versatile soul, despite its size,
is capable of unbelievable feats.
It can hover in mid-air, fly forwards, backwards,
side-ways, and even upside down.
Its rapidly beating wings can flap as high as 200 times per second,
enabling it to travel faster than a car.

The laws of physics say it should be impossible.

But the hummingbird does it anyway.

I dedicate this book to those of you
who are ready to live a life more colourful,
and to do what others may say cannot be done.

This book is also for Lorenzo, my Knight Templar,
who encourages and supports me
to make my dreams possible…

And for all my clients
who've shared their dreams with me,
and allowed me to help them achieve amazing feats.

Thank you
for inspiring me.

FREEDOM

When a bird gets free,
it does not go back for remnants
left on the bottom of the cage.

Rumi

FOREWORD

Work. It's how we spend our lives. But how many of us are spending that time wisely and happily? That's the million dollar question this book sets out to answer.

Work – at its finest – should be a wonderful form of self-expression. It was Confucius who said that once you do what you love, you'll never work again. What a great way to approach a working life. Perhaps it is the only way.

And yet for far too many of us work is just the opposite. A drudgery which drains us of energy and self-esteem. Horizons shrink and the joy of living itself seems to seep away affecting not just our hours on the job, but our lives outside of work also.

In this book, Cassandra Gaisford provides lots of insights and strategies to help many more of us reach our potential and utilise our talents.

We have known Cassandra over a number of years and have always been impressed by her boundless enthusiasm for life as it might be lived. She paints, she writes novels, she is a noted public speaker and human resources consultant.

Cassandra's entire life has been dedicated to improving the lot of the average working person by imbuing them with the conviction that work should be a fulfilling and creative endeavour aligned with our talents and values.

Is this dreaming? Read on and decide for yourself. Perhaps this book will help you to turn your dreams of a happy working life into a fulfilling reality.

—Mike Fitzsimons and Nigel Beckford, Authors of *You Don't Make a Big Leap Without a Gulp*

INTRODUCTION

"Happiness is a butterfly, which when pursued, is always just beyond your grasp, but which, if you will sit down quietly, may alight upon you."

Nathaniel Hawthorne, Novelist

It's hard to believe that I was ever unhappy at work, feeling trapped and miserable in a job that made me sick. The experience was so toxic, my central nervous system was attacked, and my confidence and self-esteem hijacked. I developed shingles and was warned I could go blind. Some of my colleagues had heart attacks. And still, they stayed.

I wanted to leave, but I doubted anyone would hire me, or that I'd ever find a job that I'd love with such a passion, that one day I would say, "This isn't work, this is fun."

I'd lost my hope, and worse, I'd lost my Self, trading in my health and happiness for the 'security' of a paycheque. I had a mortgage to feed, and a daughter to support on my own, and so I boxed on. But I started feeding my soul, like you are, by reading. And later I worked with a career coach.

As I look back on that time, I realise it's true—negative experiences can be the wake-up call you need to make an empowering change. To say, 'enough is enough' and stride forth with renewed conviction and determination to pursue your dreams.

Maybe, you feel like I once did. Wondering if being happy at work will ever happen for you. Perhaps you fear if you leave a job you hate, nobody will hire you. Or maybe you've brought into the mistaken belief that it's not realistic to expect job satisfaction. Perhaps you've been told, as I was, that you do what you love when you retire.

Or maybe you're like Sally, who has spent most of her life caring for others and supporting their dreams, their passions, their lives, that she feels overwhelmed, stressed, depressed and tired. And now menopause has struck. She can't remember the last time she felt joy.

Whether you're lost, broken-hearted, disillusioned or fed-up, that you've been drawn to this book tells me that whatever's been holding you back, you're ready to make a change for the better. You want to manifest a new career, a new life, a new reenergised, happier, younger you.

Whatever your fears or worries, your motivations or desires, you're in safe hands. I've faced those same fears, those same obstacles, the same feelings of being overwhelmed—some real, some in my mind. I've been tired, worn out mentally, emotionally, physically and spiritually. Drained financially.

But not anymore. Now, like many of my coaching and counselling clients, and people who have read my books and newspaper columns over the years, my heart's desire is now my reality. The vision I once had, inspired by these lines in a song by The Eagles, "I dream I'm on vacation, it's the perfect career for me," is now my living reality.

Equally as satisfying is the fact I've been able to share what I've learned and have guided thousands of people from a myriad of diverse backgrounds and circumstances, to find or create their own career nirvana.

I'm the founder of an internationally successful career and life coaching business and the author of a vast library of personal empowerment programs. I enjoy what I call a career combo—writing, public speaking, coaching, counselling, and training.

And I enjoy a few other creative things I do on the side. Like writing historical art-related novels, painting, and photography. And I've been blessed to meet my life partner later in life. I guess you could say, I've got it all. But I know what it's like to believe that wouldn't ever happen for me.

And I know what it's like to feel trapped. I know what it's like to doubt you'll ever be able to make a change for the better. I know what it's like to feel down, stressed and anxious. I know that in today's world when finding work is harder than ever, finding a job you love can feel like an impossible dream.

But here's the good part. I know it's possible! You can have, be, and do anything you want if you're prepared to sit quietly, and clarify what's really important to you, and put in some effort to make what you yearn for happen. So many people don't. They want the easy way out, happiness delivered to their door.

Perhaps that's why statistical research repeatedly confirms that the majority of employees are unhappy. Gallup's 2015 poll reported that only 13 percent of employees worldwide are happily engaged at work. Here's the link if you're interested in Gallup's research http://bit.ly/1O6UgLq

VALUE YOUR HAPPINESS

The statistics above are shocking. Let's change them and making the world a happier place. Happier workers are happier parents, lovers, friends, allies, colleagues, and community members. Imagine what a different world it would be if more people were happy. Be the change you want to see. In this book I'll show you how, guiding you through a step-by-step process to discover who you are and what gives you joy.

Perhaps you haven't had the time to sit down and think consciously about your career choices. Maybe, like many mid-lifers you 'just fell into' your work. Or perhaps, you've made your choices based on other people's expectations.

Do you feel stuck because you can't see any better options or don't know how to deal with obstacles preventing you from finding your best-fit career? Do you feel like Laura, heart-broken after another career disappointment, and think at 50 it's all over? Do you lack the confidence and energy to make a positive change?

All that's about to change. But first, you must prioritise your happiness, your health, and your well-being. This means making a commitment to take time out of your busy life.

Reading this book, working through the exercises designed to strengthen your self and career awareness, quietly reflecting on the things that truly matter to you, and taking inspired action will lead you to career nirvana. You'll learn how to work with joy, passion, purpose, and fulfilment—and still pay the bills!

You'll be inspired by stories of mid-lifers like you, who've found the courage to make a leap toward a better future. You can learn from Annie, who wished she'd left a job she no longer loved earlier. And Keith, who found his bliss and reclaimed his self-esteem following job loss.

Or Matt, then aged 58, who after reading this book left his job as a fed-up account director and started his own business. "*Mid-Life Career Rescue* has you thinking about what drives you, why you are doing what you are doing," he told me. "Is it making me happy, am I using my full set of skills, what can I do differently and how can I change?"

Thousands of people, many of them mid-lifers, like you, have been rescued from unfulfilling work, changed careers and found their dream jobs by implementing the tips and strategies found in this book.

You'll also read about, and be inspired by people like Jilly, who at the time of writing was in her mid-70's, and left home at 14 to make her own life and follow her bliss. Following her passion has made her ageless. Truly! I saw a photo of her taken at her most recent photography exhibition and she looked like a teenager.

What you're about to read isn't another self-help book; it's a self-empowerment book. If you're like many mid-lifers and still operating from antiquated and disempowering beliefs, the information in this book will help change your mindset. It offers ways to increase your self-knowledge. From that knowledge comes the power to take control of your life.

It is my sincerest hope that you will come to discover that many of the beliefs impacting your life are false and self-limiting, and you'll be inspired and feel empowered to change these beliefs. Like brushing your teeth, instilling empowering beliefs needs to be a daily habit.

THIS BOOK IS POWERFUL

This book is powerful. I know it is. The life I have created using this awareness is amazing. The strategies are ones I have successfully used—professionally with clients and personally during numerous self-determined, sometimes forced, reinventions.

I stand by every one of the strategies you will learn here, not just because they are grounded in strong scientific and spiritual principles, but also because I have used them to create successful turnaround, after successful turnaround, in nearly every area of my life.

Mid-Life Career Rescue is the culmination of all that I have experienced and all that I have learned, applied and successfully taught others for over two decades. I don't practice what I preach; I preach what I have practiced—because it gets results.

One thing I know for certain is that your life is too important to stay in a job you hate. You have treasures buried within you—extraordinary treasures—and so do I, and so do others. And bringing those treasures to light takes faith and focus and courage and effort. It takes a willingness to prioritise your happiness, and people to help and support you along the way. People like me and the rest of the Career Rescue Community.

WHY DID I WRITE THIS BOOK?

If you are curious about why I created *Mid-Life Career Rescue*, you may like to check out my blog posts.

The feedback I've received has also been a validation of my deepest belief that following your passion is the key to success. This combined with strengthening your creativity and imagineering skills is one of the most magical, empowering and practical things you can do to manifest your deepest desires.

Within days of its release, my first book in the *Mid-Life Career Rescue* series: '*The Call For Change*,' became a #1 bestseller on Amazon in the category of Work-Related Health. Along with Mike and Nigel's foreword, it's further confirmation of the importance I place on helping people be happy in their work. Your health is everything! Be sure to value it. Now.

SETTING YOU UP FOR SUCCESS

"Aren't you setting people up for failure?" a disillusioned career coach once challenged me when I told her my focus was not on helping people find any job but finding one that gave them joy. I couldn't help but wonder if she needed a career change.

Twenty-five years of cumulative professional experience as a career coach and counsellor, helping people work with passion and still pay the bills, answers that question. I'm setting people up for success. I'm not saying it will happen instantly, but if you follow the advice in this book, it will happen. I promise.

I've proven repeatedly with the successes I've gained for clients that thinking differently and creatively, rationally and practically, while also harnessing the power of intuition, and applying the principles of manifestation, really works. In this book, I'll show you why and how.

A large part of my philosophy and the reason behind my success with clients is my fervent belief that to achieve anything worthy in life you need to follow your passion. And I'm in good company.

As media giant Oprah Winfrey once said, "Passion is energy. Feel the power that comes from focusing on what excites you."

"New Zealander's aren't ready for passion," an international publishing company told me when I first approached them with my book idea. Incredible! Without passion, you don't have energy, and without energy you have nothing.

You have to let love, desire, and passion, not fear, or ambivalence or apathy, propel you forward. Yet worryingly, research suggests that less than 10% of people are following their passion. Perhaps that's why there is so much unhappiness in the workplace.

Don't waste another day feeling trapped. Don't be the person who spends a life of regret, or waits until they retire before they follow their passions. Don't be the person too afraid to make a change for the better, or who wishes they could lead a significant life. Make the change now. Before it's too late.

REACH FOR YOUR DREAMS

Passion, happiness, joy, fulfilment, love—call it what you will but my deepest desire is that this book encourages you to reach for your dreams, to never settle, to believe in the highest aspirations you have for yourself.

You have so many gifts, so many talents that the world so desperately needs. We need people like you who care about what they do, who want to live and work with passion and purpose.

ABOUT THIS BOOK

"All successful men and women are big dreamers. They imagine what their future could be, ideal in every respect, and then they work every day toward their distant vision, that goal or purpose."

Brian Tracy, Motivational Guru

CASSANDRA GAISFORD

WHAT MAKES YOU HAPPY?

Finding a job you love is impossible without passion, enthusiasm, zest, inspiration and the deep satisfaction that comes from doing something that delivers you some kind of buzz.

Yet, so many people have no idea what makes them happy. Working long hours, too much stress, financial strain or a whole raft of other constant pressures can soon send you drowning in a sea of negativity - robbing you of the energy and positivity you need to make a life-enhancing career change.

This book comes to your rescue. Together we'll help you get your mojo back, challenge your current beliefs and increase your sense of possibility. By tapping into a combination of practical career strategies, Law of Attraction principles, and the spiritual powers of manifestation, you'll reawaken dreams, boost your self-awareness, empower your life and challenge what you thought was possible.

We'll do this in an inspired yet structured way by strengthening your creative thinking skills, boosting your self-awareness and helping you identify your non-negotiable ingredients for career success and happiness. Little steps will lead naturally to bigger leaps, giving you the courage and confidence to take a gulp, and then fly free toward career happiness and life fulfilment.

What Makes You Happy will help you:

• Explore and clarify your passions, interests, life purpose, values, transferable skills, and natural gift and talents

• Build a strong foundation for career happiness and success by identifying your criteria for job and life satisfaction

• Value your gifts, natural knacks, and talents and confirm your work-related strengths

• Gain greater clarity about what you want to change and how to direct your energies positively toward your preferred future

• Strengthen your creative thinking skills, and ability to identify possible roles you would enjoy, including self-employment

• Have the courage to quit, or fall back in love with a job you've come to hate

• Take the stress out of worrying you'll make the wrong move, and super-charge the confidence needed to make an inspired change

• Shift ingrained, sabotaging beliefs by tapping into the realms where science meets spirituality

• Find your point of brilliance

Let's look briefly at what each chapter in this book will cover.

Chapter One, "Pursue Your Passion Not Your Pension," will help you discover the things you are passionate about. Tapping into your passion will help ignite untapped gifts and talents. It will also help you to unleash latent potential. Re-inspired, you'll begin the process of identifying how your passion can turn into a rewarding and fulfilling career.

So many people have a mistaken belief you can't do what you love and get paid. Real stories of people and organisations that have achieved success by doing something they believe deeply in, and have a talent for will challenge that. Equally life-enhancing is making time for hobbies you enjoy. You may find you fall back in love with a job you've come to hate when you get some balance back.

Chapter two, "Inspiration Used to Carve Out an Opportunity," will highlight the role your deepest interests have in finding or creating work you will love.

It's incredible when I recall my experience working in a globally renown outplacement agency, helping people rebuild their lives after a job loss, that the career coaching programs they were offered never encouraged people to evaluate their interests. How can you possibly be happy at work if your job doesn't interest you?

Chapter Three, "Get the Edge, Find Your Purpose," shows you how to harness the motivating power of living and working with a purpose. Clarifying the things that give your life meaning and purpose will help you tap into latent ambitions and desires, and identify career options that will be deeply fulfilling.

This chapter will also help you to make sense of past and current experiences and use these to clarify the work you were born to do. This is a place of real alchemy—negatives will be turned into positives. You'll see!

Chapter Four, "Prioritising What's Important," emphasises how critical it is to find or create work that aligns with your most important values. Values conflicts are the most common cause of unhappiness at work and workplace stress. Yet research confirms that many people don't even know what their values or needs are.

The exercises in this chapter will help you identify and prioritise your most important career values and apply them to career decision-making. If work is stressing you out, you'll also gain some tips to try to get your values met before you quit.

Many people think that unless they have a formal qualification or recent work experience, they don't have any skills. **Chapter Five, "Valuing Natural Knacks and Talents,"** will boost awareness of your natural gifts and innate abilities and strengths.

As one of my clients who hated her job told me, "I'm good at what I do, and people keep promoting me but does anybody ask me if enjoy it?" Importantly, this chapter will also help you to identify your favourite skills and the activities that bring you joy.

Chapter Six, "Strategies To Improve Happiness At Work," will help you identify ways to re-engineer your work to better meet your needs. You'll also benefit from strategies to help boost self-esteem and confidence, and believe in who you are and what you do.

Mid-Life Career Rescue: What Makes You Happy, concludes with showing you how to identify your point of brilliance. I've also included a link to a free workbook to help you improve your decision-making and take the stress out of choosing your best-fit career.

HOW TO USE THIS BOOK

The key components of determining what you want to do and what others will pay you to do are presented in bite-sized portions that make it much easier to assimilate.

Journal exercises, inspiring quotations, and many other simple but effective tools to feed your inspiration and boost your confidence will help feed your desire for a new, improved life.

Throughout this book, you'll be encouraged to make positive changes in your life, step by step, by applying the strategies discussed. You may want to create a special journal, notebook or use a digital tool to make a few notes and apply the tools and techniques I've designed especially for you.

My aim is to make *Mid-Life Career Rescue* as interactive as possible by combining a minimum of theory with a maximum of practical tools, techniques and inspiring stories from other successful career-changers that you can apply to your own situation.

YOUR VIRTUAL COACH

To really benefit from this book think of it as your 'virtual' coach—try the action tasks and additional exercises that you'll find in all the chapters.

These action tasks are designed to facilitate greater insight and to help you integrate new learnings. Resist the urge to just process them in your head. We learn best by doing. Research has repeatedly proven that the act of writing deepens your knowledge and learning.

For example, a study conducted by Dr. David K. Pugalee found that journal writing was an effective instructional tool and aided learning. His research found that writing helped people organise and describe internal thoughts and thus improve their problem-solving skills.

Henriette Klauser, Ph.D., also provides compelling evidence in her book, *Write It Down And Make It Happen*, that writing helps you clarify what you want and enables you to make it happen.

Writing down your insights is the area where people like motivational guru Tony Robbins, say that the winners part from the losers because the losers always find a reason not to write things down. Harsh but perhaps true!

You will also come across plenty of action questions. Open-ended questions are great thought provokers. Your answers to these questions will help you gently challenge current assumptions and gain greater clarity about your goals and desires.

If you are unemployed, or not in paid work, you may find it helpful to think about any previous roles or life experiences when completing the exercises.

KEEPING A PASSION JOURNAL

A passion journal is also a great place to store sources of inspiration to support you through the career planning and change process. For some tips to help you create your own inspirational passion journal, go to the media page on my website and watch my television interview, or purchase my popular book, The Passion Journal: The Effortless Path to Manifesting Your Love, Life, and Career Goals. You'll find loads of help and inspiration in these pages.

If you need more help to find and live your life purpose you may prefer to take my online course and watch inspirational and practical videos and other strategies to help you fulfil your potential. You'll find details at the end of this book.

PASSION JOURNAL TIP SHEET

Every year I create a passion journal to help clarify and manifest my intentions. It's a fun and incredibly powerful process. I've created my dream job, a soul mate, our wonderful lifestyle property, a publishing contract and more. Try it for yourself!

INSPIRATIONAL QUOTES

Sometimes all it takes is the slightest encouragement—one simple inspirational sentence—to launch oneself into a new and more satisfying orbit. I have included plenty of inspiration throughout the book and in the Career Rescue Community detailed below to help you do just that!

SURF THE NET

Throughout the book, I have included a selection of my e-Resources. These have been carefully selected to encourage further insight and to enable you to tap into regularly updated resources, including those created by me just for you.

There is no 'right' or 'wrong' way to work with *Mid-Life Career Rescue*. It's a very flexible tool—the only requirement is that you use it in a way that meets your needs. For example, you may wish to work through the book and exercises sequentially. Alternatively, you may wish to work intuitively and complete the exercises in an ad hoc fashion. Or just start where you need to start.

While it is recommended that the chapters and the exercises are worked through in the order they appear, each chapter can be read independently. You may wish to read a chapter each week, fortnight or month. Or you may wish to use your intuition and select a page at random.

GETTING STARTED

Increasing your self-awareness is a crucial first step in moving toward the career of your dreams. Take the time to complete the following Happy At Work Quiz to evaluate where you are now.

HAPPY AT WORK QUIZ

- You're passionate about what you do

- Your work gives your life meaning and purpose

- Your career helps you achieve your long-term goals

- Your life is in balance—family, love, spirituality, health, relaxation, money, altruism, friendships, and hobbies

- Work fulfils your deepest, driving interests

- Your personal and career values are satisfied

- The skills you enjoy using and give you a buzz are valued

- People appreciate the work you do and you receive positive feedback

- You know how your skills and passions can transfer into different careers if you ever wanted to, or needed to change your job

- Workplace stress is managed proactively and wellness is encouraged

• You enjoy your relationships with the people you work with

• Career development opportunities exist and you feel you can learn and grow

• Your salary or income is enough to meet your needs

• You are personally growing and developing—you're clear about the things that hold you back and have developed a strategy to minimise these weaknesses

• You feel confident and have healthy self-esteem

• Your career takes you closer toward achieving your long-term goals

• You're respected, trusted and your ideas are listened to

• You enjoy a reasonable amount of freedom and autonomy

• You know how to use your strengths to minimise your weaknesses

• If you're unhappy at work you know how to identify the source of your unhappiness and what steps you need to take to make a change for the better

• Your work allows you to be yourself

Scoring:

If you answered "yes" to 14 or more of these statements you have a great level of enjoyment in your work and are really clear about what drives your career happiness.

If you answered "yes" to more than six but less than 14 of these statements, you are less happy at work and would benefit from gaining more self-awareness about your criteria for job satisfaction and alternative career options.

If you only answered "yes" to five or less of these statements, at least you now have a better idea of what you need to be happy. Sometimes in life, as in photography, you need a negative to make a positive.

By building greater self and career awareness in those areas where you answered "no," and channeling your energies into finding ways to get your needs met, you'll build excitement, confidence and identify career options that you will enjoy and be good at.

Once you are clear about what you need to be happy at work and the forces that drive your decisions, finding a job that you like is easy. It won't happen overnight but it will happen! The exercises in the book will show you how.

GETTING READY FOR CHANGE

As I shared in my first book *The Call For Change* the greatest thing you can do to fast-track your success is to strengthen your creative thinking skills. I also shared the importance of maintaining a child-like curiosity and being open-minded.

Patience, faith, and trust are also important qualities to cultivate during the change process. You don't want to rush off down a career path you later regret, or miss looking into something that could have been fulfilling, because you weren't clear about your criteria for career satisfaction, or were in a hurry to find your happy place.

You don't need to have read *Mid-Life Career Rescue: The Call For Change* to benefit from this book. My first book focuses specifically on helping people build greater awareness of the positive aspects of being a mid-lifer, and how to boost their creative thinking skills.

Crucially, it also amplifies the importance of preparing a solid foundation for positive change by reducing stress and building greater resilience—before it's too late. If these things are impacting you, it may be another helpful tool in your happiness kit.

Mid-Life Career Rescue: What Makes You Happy, turbo boosts your self-awareness—especially in clarifying the things you need to be really happy at work. It goes deeper into exploring your passions, your values, skills and natural talents and life purpose.

The result is to leave you with a checklist to aid decision making. This will take the stress out of worrying you'll make the wrong move, and super-charge the confidence needed to make an inspired change.

In saying that, it's hard to feel inspired, impossible to be creative, and challenging to feel confident if you're stressed out of your mind, or believe you're too old to change. If you haven't read *Mid-Life Career Rescue: The Call For Change* I feel it would help.

Get ready for change by cultivating a sense of adventure and bring your whole self to the journey. Keep your head in the clouds, your feet on the ground, think with your heart and feel with your head, and stay flexible and have fun. With the right attitude reinventing your career and your life can be a truly enlightening experience.

Have faith in yourself and your capacity for reinvention and remember you're not starting at the beginning. You already have a wealth of skills and knowledge, and life experience to draw upon.

When you allow your passion to guide, motivate and inspire you the possibilities are endless. We have entered the era of the older worker. Growing numbers of 40-plus men and women are taking up new challenges and redefining their careers every day. Now more than ever you can be, do and have nearly anything you desire.

Are you ready to find out what makes you happy and transform your life?

I

PURSUE YOUR PASSION NOT YOUR PENSION

JOB DISSATISFACTION

"When you are inspired by some great purpose, some extraordinary project, all your thoughts break their bonds. Your mind transcends limitations, your consciousness expands in every direction, and you find yourself in a new, great and wonderful world. Dormant forces, faculties and talents become alive, and

you discover yourself to be a greater person by far than you ever dreamed yourself to be."

Patanjali, Yogi and Mystic

A healthy obsession can be a liberating and clarifying catalyst to your true calling and career direction—especially for people in the mid-life zone. With maturity comes renewed confidence and determination to pursue the things they are truly passionate about.

FULLY ALIVE

Being passionate is a vital part of being human. Passion is love—hard to define, but easy to see and feel when it is alive. Passion is about emotion, feeling, zest and enthusiasm. Intensity, fervour, ardor, and zeal. Passion is about fire, eagerness, and preoccupation.

Passion is about excitement and animation. Passion is about determination and self-belief. Passion is about being willing to change. Passion is about following your heart's desire. Passion is about doing something you love.

It's not an intellectual thought. It's a feeling. Feelings matter, and feelings are where the real power is. But Western society tends to predominately value thoughts, reason, logic and clear thinking more highly than feelings, intuition, spirit, and soul.

Perhaps because of this, people have become desensitised to the clues and callings of their own passions.

Some of the strategies I'll share with you in this book may be criticised as 'fluff' or 'snake oil.' People often fear that which they don't understand. I was attacked in this vein when I once offered a doctor some lavender oil to help reduce her mental strain. But understand this, the heart has its own reasons, its own desires, its own magical way of making itself heard.

Passion, some say, can be difficult to find, but if you're awake it will find you. Stay open-hearted and open-minded. Don't be like so many adults who fail to discover it at all, and in the absence of any encouragement, give up.

"People pride themselves upon their willpower, their indomitable courage, upon the fact that nothing frightens them," writes T. Lobsang Rampa, in his classic book, *You Forever.* "They assured bored listeners that with their willpower they can do anything at all."

But the truth is there is no greater power than imagination, passion, and the incredible power of love.

If you are serious about being happy, if it's your desire to be the best that you can be, then the integration of your mind, body, and spirit is essential. Make a commitment to working and living with passion—I'll show you where to look!

PASSION'S PAY CHEQUE

Pursuing your passion can be profitable on many levels:

✓ When you do what you love, your true talent will reveal itself; passion can't be faked

✓ You will be more enthusiastic about your pursuits

✓ You will have more energy to overcome obstacles

✓ You will be more determined to make things happen

✓ You will enjoy your work

✓ Your work will become a vehicle for self-expression

✓ Passion will give you a competitive edge

New Zealand motorcycling legend Burt Munro proved that passion is the key to success. "All my life I've wanted to do something big," he said. In 1967 Burt achieved something huge.

At the age of 68, against all the odds, he set a world record of 183.586 mph with his highly modified Indian Scout motorcycle. To qualify he made a one-way run of 190.07 mph, the fastest ever officially recorded speed on an Indian.

Like so many inspiring people the road to success was not an easy one—it involved much personal hardship and numerous setbacks, but armed with his passion and a compelling desire to "go out with a bang," Burt Munro mortgaged his house and set out on the greatest adventure of his life.

His truly awesome achievements were bought to life in an inspiring and uplifting film, *The World's Fastest Indian*.

The World's Fastest Indian not only gives movie-goers an inside look at Munro's passion, but it also gives them an idea of New Zealand filmmaker Roger Donaldson's overwhelming desire to tell the story.

"This project has been a passion of mine since I completed a documentary about Burt Munro back in 1972," Donaldson said. "I have been intrigued by Burt's story for many, many years; some would say my obsession with this film matches Burt's obsession with his bike."

Donaldson's passion for his subject has won him international acclaim from Academy Award-winning actor Anthony Hopkins. "I thought it was a terrific movie. It is a unique script... it is just so well written, very well written, beautifully written, and so refreshing. I've worked with a lot of great directors, Steven Spielberg, and

Oliver Stone, and Roger Donaldson is there with that lot, you know. He really is," Hopkins said.

OBSESSIONS BOOST HEALTH

A healthy obsession can lead you to many things, including your:

1) **Life niche**—creating a breath of fresh air and giving you a competitive edge

2) **True bliss**—leading you to your vocation where being paid is the icing on the cake

3) **Your point of excellence**—unleashing dormant talents and natural gifts

4) **Your life purpose**—spreading seeds of joy and inspiration and benefiting others.

AUTHENTIC HAPPINESS: LOVE IS WHERE THE MAGIC IS

Love is where the magic is. When you love what you do with such a passion you'd do it for free, this is your path with heart. You've heard the saying, 'when you do what you love, you'll never work again.' It's true. Work doesn't feel like a slog, it feels energising.

From Teacher to Romance Writer

As Annie Featherston, writing as Sophia James, shares below, when you combine your favourite skills with doing something you completely and utterly love, you come home to your true Self and find your place of bliss. The result? Contentment—and more often than not, producing something highly marketable.

"I'd taught for fifteen years and loved it. And then I didn't.

19

It wasn't the students or the workload. It wasn't the noise or the constant worry of, 'was I doing enough' that pushed me out either.

I was a good teacher but underneath was a passion that I couldn't ignore any longer. I wanted to be writer, a historical romance writer, and I was beginning to get offered some wonderful opportunities that did not meld with the structured teaching year and the constant pressure of it.

I felt like a juggler with a hundred balls in the air. I was teaching half time, taking tours to Europe with my husband to help him, running mentorship programs.... and writing.

Writing was my complete and utter love and yet it was always taking a secondary place. I wrote at night. I wrote in the weekends. I wrote when the kids were asleep. When I wrote I didn't think of the time or the problems, all I saw was the joy and passion of it. I loved forming characters and thinking of stories. I lay in bed at night asking my protagonists questions and spent many hours trawling over history books to place them into a context.

I have a degree in history so it was as if all the things I had enjoyed were coming together at last. History and writing. I knew that at 54 I couldn't be patient any longer.

I needed to be in a field that I felt fully aware in, that I loved beyond the weekly paycheque and that filled my spirit with lightness.

I'd just won a New Zealand based competition for a completed romance and it was validation, I suppose. If I didn't make the jump and do it now perhaps I never would. And if I never gave myself a chance I would feel bereft.

I penned my resignation letter and left to Australia to be a mentor on a five-day intensive scheme the Romance Writers of Australia were running. It was scary and hard but when I finished it successfully I remember standing alone in front of the mirror, a cold sore from exhaustion and worry on my lip, but my clenched fist punching the air in triumph.

To feel like that is to know you live.

When I got picked up by Harlequin Historical and published it felt like all the dreams I had hoped for so long were finally happening. I had visualised this. I had walked the lonely windy beaches of Gisborne and shouted my hopes for it into the wind. I had sat in the mall with three crying children in the car and written scenarios on the back of the supermarket docket because the story just wouldn't wait until I got home.

If I had not been paid one cent for my writing I would still have done it somehow. But the strange thing is that money does follow passion and suddenly I was making as much as I ever did in part-time teaching.

Writing is hard work. A book does not come fully formed from thin air or dreams for me. But I've persevered and sat and written. I've made deadlines. I've written blogs. I have delved into social media and stood there with a smile on my face when the reviews have not been what I wanted.

But I have always believed in myself and my stories. I've kept going. I have never given up.

And I have loved my writing life, my freedom, the creativity, the possibilities.

If I had my time over I would have left my teaching career earlier. I would have been braver and less worried by all the sensible advice others were giving me. I should have listened to my heart and taken the jump into a lifestyle that is my perfect fit and even if I had never succeeded I would have known that at least I tried."

I love Annie's story of reinvention. So-called sensible advice is no replacement for the wisdom of your heart, your soul, your intuitive knowing about what choices are right for you.

"When you show a bit of courage, The Universe rewards you." ~ Laurie Wills, Change-maker

Action Task! Find Your Passion

Real passion is more than a fad or a fleeting enthusiasm. It can't be turned on and off like a tap. Answering the following questions will help you begin to clarify the things you are most passionate about:

1) When does time seem to fly? When was the last time you felt really excited, or deeply absorbed in, or obsessed by, something? What were you doing? Who were you with? What clues did you notice?

2) What do you care deeply or strongly about? Discovering all the things that you believe in is not always easy. Look for the clues to your deep beliefs by catching the times you use words such as 'should' or 'must.'

3) What do you value? What do you need to experience, feel, or be doing to feel deeply fulfilled?

4) What pushes your buttons or makes you angry? How could you use your anger constructively to bring about change?

5) Which skills and talents come most easily or naturally to you? Which ones give you a buzz or a huge sense of personal satisfaction?

6) What inspires you? Passion goes in all directions. It could be as tangible as a job or a person, or as intangible as a dream or an idea. List all your obsessions and the things that interest you deeply. If you're struggling to identify your interests and inspirations, you'll find some handy prompts in the next chapter

7) Keep a passion journal. It's staggeringly, and dishearteningly, true that many people don't know what they are passionate about, or how they can turn it into a rewarding career. Some research suggests that only 10% of people are living and working with passion. Hence my passion for passion - to bring about positive change in the world. Creating a passion journal is one simple but powerful technique to help achieve this.

This is where manifesting your preferred future really happens. I've been keeping a passion journal for years and so many things I've visualised and affirmed on the pages, are now my living realities.

Client Success Story: From Manager to Visual Merchandiser

Jane wanted to change her profession from a background in retail sales and management to something more creative and hands-on. She was struggling to identify how her passion for fabric could be combined into a new career.

I encouraged her to gather clues to her preferred future, by collecting examples of others who enjoyed successful careers working with fabrics. She began a passion journal, which she covered with her favourite fabric, and regularly updated her journal with aspirational images, inspirational quotes, confirmation of her strengths and clues to her passion.

After focusing on all the facets of her passion, including her natural gifts and talents, the laws of manifestation, focus and intention kicked into gear, and she successfully transitioned into her dream job.

"I have just been offered the position of visual merchandiser for a furnishings chain. This job is going to enable me to use all those key skills that I have and a huge bonus is that I also get to work with fabrics, which is just perfect. I know I came across with confidence and the right attitude thanks to you reminding me that I need to 'blow my own trumpet' and allow my passion to shine."

Jane's story is a powerful reminder of how you can manifest your preferred future by making passion your priority, allowing no doubt and visualising your dreams into reality.

WHAT WERE YOUR CHILDHOOD DREAMS?

"Persevere with your mid-life, bring into consciousness your childhood dreams for they will become your living realities."

~Max Gimblett, Artist, and Zen Buddhist Monk

At the age of eight, Donna Hay skipped into a kitchen, picked up a mixing bowl and never looked back. She later moved into the world of magazine test kitchens and publishing, where she established her signature style of simple, smart and seasonal recipes—all beautifully photographed.

Her unique style turned her into one of the first celebrity chefs—an international food-publishing phenomenon and best-selling author. Like many passionate business people, Donna has many outlets all unified by her abiding passion for food. Along with publishing cookbooks and producing her own magazine, she's created a line of homewares, a food range, and at the time of print, now has her own general store.

Many experts say that your passion reveals itself early on in your life. If you're lucky, someone close to you will have noticed your natural inclination and encouraged you towards your true vocation.

Chances are, you weren't that lucky. Many baby-boomers weren't encouraged to follow their childhood bliss. Pay it no mind. It's not too late to follow it now.

Action Questions: What did you love as a child?

What were your childhood dreams? What did you love to do as a child? What steps can you take to make these your living reality? Perhaps a hobby could be a stepping-stone toward a new career.

As you contemplate making changes in your life, how can you maintain a spirit of curiosity, and allow yourself to be childlike?

Never Grow Up

"...stay in part a child, with the creativity and invention that characterises children before they are deformed by adult society."

~ Jean Piaget, Educational Psychologist

"When will you grow up?" asks Jenny Regels' husband, affectionately. While visiting Russell in the astoundingly beautiful Bay Of Islands in New Zealand, I had the great fortune of wandering into Jenny's crystal and spiritual haven—aptly named *'Peace and Plenty.'*

We immediately connected and I had a great time 'playing' with one of the many pendulums she has for sale. I gained confirmation from Spirit that the choices I was considering were right.

When Jenny, then a youthful 69-year-old, shared with me the great joy she feels every day being childlike I asked her if she'd share a few words of wisdom with those of us, who at times, take life too seriously.

"It's really, really important not to grow up, and to keep a young mind and be interested in everything going on around you. And keep your inner child active the whole time. Really active. And keep

25

a positive outlook on life. Don't be the glass half empty person. Be the one-half full. Always."

I left feeling uplifted, reaffirmed in the knowledge that I want what Jenny's got—ageless grace, peace and plenty.

Surf The Net

Take a peek inside Jenny's crystal haven and listen to this delightful, ageless lady here https://vimeo.com/147984220

Tune Into Your Body Barometer

As Neale Walsch, the author of *Conversations With God*, says, "Judge not about which you feel passionate. Simply notice it, then see if it serves you, given who and what you wish to be."

Notice the times you feel a sense of excitement, a state of arousal, a feeling of limitless energy, a burning desire, a strong gut feeling, a feeling of contentment, strong emotions or determination. Notice these feelings and record them in your passion journal.

During my time in the United States, I was very lucky to have been able to stay in New York and to visit the Metropolitan Museum of Art. I was even luckier because while I was there I unexpectedly rediscovered a passion I had forgotten.

I share the following excerpt from my passion journal at that time (which incidentally was bright red!), in the hope that it illustrates some of the strategies I am encouraging you to try.

"To see these paintings makes my heart sing, my eyes sparkle, and a smile settle upon my lips. I feel a shortness of breath and my heart rate quickens. I want to take them all in and love the ones with texture so rich you can almost feel the paint. I have to stop myself from reaching out to touch them. I am flushed with excitement and a thirst that cannot be quenched."

And so it was that my 'body barometer' reminded me of the deep joy and love I feel when I paint with oil. I had traded my passion for the convenience of acrylic, but I found it joyless and plastic.

I thought it was a great confirmation of the power of passion when an art gallery owner, who bought some of my paintings not long after I returned from New York, said to me, "You have a rare ability to capture an emotion."

I later won the Supreme Art Award for an oil painting I did of my grandmother. It was the first portrait I had ever painted. I'm not a formally trained artist, more of a dabbler. So yes, magic can happen when you follow your passion.

"YOU MUST FIRST BE who you really are, then do what you really need to do, in order to have what you want."

~ Margaret Young, Singer and Comedienne

DISSATISFACTION QUIZ

As I shared in the first book in the *Mid-Life Career Rescue* series, *The Call for Change,* before you find the cure to your job blues you first need to get clear about what's causing the problem. The following Dissatisfaction Quiz will help.

Perhaps you can identify with some of the common causes of dissatisfaction below. In your journal record (or highlight in your eBook) the statements below that are true for you.

You may find that this is a useful starting point in identifying what needs to change in order to be happy at work.

Your answers can also highlight which parts or books in the series will be most helpful to you.

1. You don't know what your skills are or what you're good at
2. Lack of recognition—people don't value you and what you do

bored and your job lacks challenge—you can't see
opportunity for growth or advancement

culture is very negative

5. You don't get on with your co-workers
6. You feel stuck and can't see a way to make any improvements
7. You keep getting looked over for promotion
8. You don't know what makes you happy
9. You're not doing the things that really matter to you
10. The job doesn't meet your values
11. Your life feels out of balance
12. The workload is too heavy
13. Your job pays the bills but your passions are left as a hobby
14. You have a growing sense—vague though it might be—that you could improve the quality of your life
15. You have very little autonomy and control over your work
16. Your role or organisation isn't spiritually aligned to the things you believe in
17. Office politics get you down
18. Your job and/or work environment is not fun
19. People don't have pride in their work, and poor performance is often ignored
20. Your wages are too low
21. The organisation is too bureaucratic—policies and procedures slow everything down
22. You're not using the skills you enjoy
23. You feel 'boxed' in and don't know how to get into something different
24. You don't know what you want to do
25. Only the bosses' ideas are listened to
26. Your job lacks security
27. Very little about the job interests you
28. You have lost your confidence and your self-esteem is low

29. You're not achieving your potential
30. You park the 'real you' at the door—the robotic you goes to work
31. Personal issues are impacting on your enjoyment of work —these issues affect your focus, and motivation, etc.
32. The work environment isn't very attractive
33. Lack of training and support makes it difficult to do your job well
34. People are bullied and/or not treated with respect
35. Your role lacks meaning and purpose—you don't feel that what you contribute makes a difference

SCORING:

0-6 Congratulations! Nothing really seems to be getting you down. Perhaps you're just looking for a new challenge. Read on for tips and strategies to help you move in a new direction.

6-20 IF YOU ANSWERED "YES" to 6 or more of these statements you are moderately dissatisfied with the way things are going in your life. Develop specific actions for identifying and incorporating passion into your life.

21-35 YOU ARE SUFFERING from severe dissatisfaction. You really do deserve to pursue a more satisfying alternative. Take immediate steps now to create positive changes in your work and life. In addition to applying the strategies in this book, you may wish to solicit the support of a professional.

WHAT YOU'VE LEARNED SO FAR

- Passion is energy. It is emotion, zest, intensity, enthusiasm, and excitement. Passion is love.
- Do what inspires you! Pursuing your passion, not your pension, can be a liberating and clarifying catalyst to your true calling and best-fit career.
- A healthy obsession can lead to many things. Not only will

your passion lead you to your path with heart, it will also help fuel the fires of self-belief, determination, and courage. You'll be fully alive, stand out from the crowd and gain a competitive edge.

- If you don't know where to look passion can be difficult to find. Tune into your body barometer and notice the times when you feel most alive, inspired, or fulfilled.

- Start a passion journal. Keep track of the times when you notice clues to your passion, such as a feeling of inspiration or any of the other signs discussed in this chapter. Record these moments in an inspirational journal so that they don't get lost or forgotten.

- Gain greater awareness of what drives your passion by asking yourself, "Why am I passionate about this?" Look for the themes and patterns. Keep your passion alive by updating your journal and referring to it regularly. Actively look for jobs and examples of people who have made the things you are passionate about into a rewarding career and life. Keep generating ideas about how you could add more passion in your life.

WHAT'S NEXT?

In the next chapter, you'll discover how joyous, and exciting work and life is when you're following your obsessions and doing what interests and inspires you.

"I believe the greatest tool I developed was an unwavering decision to commit my full energy to my Heart's desire. I learned to organise my life around my dream, rather than try and force my dream into my chaotic life."

~ Sonia Choquette, Psychic Intuitive and Author

II

GET THE EDGE FIND YOUR PURPOSE

PRIORITIZING WHAT'S IMPORTANT

"Values are a matter of what guides you through every day, every task, every encounter with another human being. Yet we are often unaware of what our values are."

Richard Bolles, Author

Sometimes the job of your dreams may be the one least likely to pay the most. But it's not always about the money, right? There's more to being rewarded for the work you do than the paycheque you take home at the end of the week.

Job satisfaction, fulfilment, quality of family and private life and mental, spiritual, physical, and emotional health are too often left out of the equation when evaluating job opportunities.

Most people will say that having enough money to live comfortably is important to them. But not everyone is willing to work for less money in order to have other needs met.

For these people what they value most is not money, it's something else more important to them - such as working for a specific cause, helping people, being creative, being challenged or having great work-life balance and plenty of free time.

Being aware of what your non-negotiable values are, and proactively ensuring these needs are met at work is vitally important. A career choice that is in line with your core beliefs and values is more likely to be a lasting and positive choice. It allows you to be who you really are, and do what you really need, in order to achieve what you want.

WHAT ARE VALUES?

Your most important values are the things you feel very strongly about. Your values are who you are and who you want to be. They are the ideals that guide or qualify your personal conduct, interaction with others and involvement in your career.

Like morals, they help you to distinguish what is right from what is wrong, and what is good from what makes you feel terrible. They're signposts which direct you to your best-fit career and inform you on how you can live your life in a meaningful way.

Your values are formed in a variety of ways through your life experiences, the way you are uniquely wired and the choices you make. They're who you are and who you choose to be.

Jilly left home when she was only 14. As she says, hers was not a conventional life. Now in her 70's, her most important values centre around independence, autonomy, creativity, and freedom. It's not hard to understand why. Now living in a medieval village near to Menton, France, and working as a photographer and journalist, her life and work reflect who she is and the things most important to her.

Listening to Jilly's stories of reinvention, it's clear to me that variety, learning and new challenges are important values too.

"I've always followed my dream - I wasn't a mid-lifer who found what I wanted to do. I always took chances and jumped in with both feet! I ran a drama school with a one-time husband, I was an actress, I owned two restaurants, one in London, one in Hobart, Tasmania.

My grand passion though was dogs and bred and showed dogs for over thirty years and during the 1980s, had one of the top breeding and showing kennels in Old English Sheepdogs. I also judged the breed all over the world. I've lived in America, in Australia, in Wales, in London, and, for the past 25 years, in France. I was never ever a person who needed a mid-life boost as it were."

Jilly, says she always had what others call courage. In fact, had I not said 'yes' to every opportunity in life I knew I'd always worry what I'd missed. It seemed to me it took more courage to say, 'No' than to say, 'Yes'." When she was 67, new adventures beckoned, and she picked up a camera.

I didn't get into photography because it was something I'd always wanted to do—in fact, during my years showing Old English Sheepdogs I was endlessly taking photos of the show dogs and puppies, so perhaps that was the beginning of my creativity in photography.

But about eight years ago a blog about a town not far from me drew my attention, and I thought 'I can do that!' and so I did. My photography was woeful - crooked buildings, and horizons - not that I knew it at the time. But slowly by looking at other photographer's work, I started to 'see' what I needed to improve. I got inspired and gradually improved my skills (I still am!).

I took workshops, (Carla Coulson and Nick Danziger - both life-changing) photography friends helped me, I read endlessly on the subject and watched training videos. Eventually, instead of writing about my town with photos, I was taking photos for their own sake.

I do think life experiences have made me a better photographer —the technical side had to be learned, but it's in what I choose to photograph that defines my work. I love, for instance, the world of street photography. For me, a good photograph needs to make the photographer and the viewer 'feel' something."

I love Jilly's motivation, 'I could do that!' How many times have you said that? But how many times have you acted on it?

Jilly's most recent creative endeavour blends her love for dogs with her passion for photography. "During my years as a dog breeder, exhibitor and judge, I always photographed my dogs in show pose. I think that gave me an 'eye' for a photo, as I had an eye for a dog, as we say."

Check out her website (http://www.jillybennett.com)—her work is really, really special. Her natural affinity for dogs and the skills she's developed with the camera creates something truly magical. She has now had several exhibitions with two more coming up next year. She has also been invited to join Getty Images.

Jilly is currently working on two books, one about the medieval hill village where she lives - not a book for tourists, as such, but one that will follow the daily lives of the people who live there and who have made her so welcome. The second book will be called *Riviera Dogs*.

SAYING YES TO OPPORTUNITIES MAKES YOUR LIFE RICHER

As Jilly's story highlights saying 'yes' to opportunities as they appear has made her life richer. I recall a similar point of choice when I was asked to work in some of the most dangerous New Zealand prisons. My first reaction was born of fear.

I thought of all the possible things that could go wrong—even imagining myself being assaulted by prisoners. Initially, I tried to talk my manager out of hiring me. "What makes you think I'd be right for this role?"

She looked at me, a grin on her face, and said, "They'll see this pretty wee thing, and think they can manipulate you, and then they'll meet that rod of steel."

"What rod of steel?" I wondered. Not only did my manager see qualities in me that I hadn't seen, but she also recognised the value I place on creating positive outcomes. And she sensed I had the metal to do what needed to be done—not aggressively, but by building trust and rapport.

Looking back, I'm glad I took the contract. It would have been easy to say, 'no' and stay in the comfort rut. But living my values, and my love of a challenge and transforming lives helped me say, 'yes.' The role also received a big tick because my manager gave me loads, and loads of autonomy and the freedom to make decisions.

A six-month contract coaching senior managers and helping transform the culture of New Zealand Prisons stretched into three years, and it was one of the most memorable and rewarding work experiences of my life.

ACTION QUESTION: WHAT COULD YOU SAY, 'YES' TO?

What opportunities or possibilities might you be able to say yes to?

If you can't think of anything right now to say 'yes' to, you may find it easier to say, 'no.' No to staying in a job you no longer love. No to a job that makes you sick. No! No! No—to situations, people and circumstances that don't bring out the best in you and feed your soul.

You don't need to be harsh or reckless to say no. You don't need to feel guilty or fearful either. Be strong. Do what empowers you.

Do what liberates you. Do what makes you feel good. Choose love not fear, consider your options from all angles and plan for the best outcome, and all else will follow.

. . .

BY SAYING NO, you've just said, 'yes!' Yes, to living your values.

"YOUR LIFE IS RIGHT NOW! It's not later! It's not in that time of retirement. It's not when the lover gets here. It's not when you've moved into the new house. It's not when you get the better job. Your life is right now. It will always be right now. You might as well decide to start enjoying your life right now, because it's not ever going to get better than right now-until it gets better right now!" ~ Abraham Hicks

ACTION TASK! VALUES@WORK CHECKLIST

Do you understand the need to honour your personal values, but struggle to identify those most important to you at work? Clarifying and prioritising your values is one of the most important steps you will take when assessing your career.

To help gain awareness of your work values, complete the following checklist. Going on instinct or gut-feel, rate items according to the importance that you place on them in your life today.

Add to this list any values that are personally meaningful to you. As you are doing this exercise you may find it helpful to recall what you experienced in situations when your values were met, and in situations when your values weren't met.

Step 1: Prioritise your values

Rate the following values from 1 to 5 in terms of what's most important to you:

5 is really important and 1 is least important.

- Time freedom   5

- Innovation 4
- Change and variety u
- Working with others *Depends*
- Working alone 3
- Having fun 5
- Artistic creativity
- Job tranquility
- Being physically active 5
- High earnings
- Helping others
- Meaning and purpose
- Challenge
- Achieving excellence 5
- Leadership
- Prestige and status
- Love
- Passion
- Being an expert 5
- Work-life balance 5
- Friendship u
- Spirituality 4
- Respect 5
- Competition 3
- Fast pace
- Other: generate your own list

Step 2: Choose your 7 most important values

Narrow your most important values to 7. These are the most important needs a job needs to fulfil for you to be happy and productive.

Step 3: Describe your 7 most important values

Help make your values concrete and personally meaningful by describing what each value means to you.

For example, independence is important to me. It means many things to me: autonomy, financial freedom, creative control, making decisions and working collaboratively, but independently towards my goals. It's why working for myself, and helping others achieve their goals, works so well for me.

GET REAL ABOUT WHAT'S IMPORTANT

"The things that matter most should not be sacrificed to those that matter least."

~ Dr Stephen R. Covey, Author

Values conflicts are one of the major causes of work-related stress. If you're proactive you'll get out unscathed, and as you'll read later in this chapter, not getting your needs met may just lead you to your life purpose.

"I used to be the sort of person who usually put her head down and worked towards a goal and if I worked hard enough and aimed for my goal, then success would follow. And for the first time my life plan wasn't working out," said Juliet de Baubigny, a powerful venture capitalist in Silicon Valley. Her entrepreneurial genius is said to have contributed to the transformation of companies such as Google and Amazon.

Several years ago her marriage ended in a bitter divorce, her young son was diagnosed with Type I diabetes, and she ended up in the ICU with bilateral pneumonia, all within six months. "It makes you question faith and humanity," she said. "So I thought how do I redirect this?"

Juliet heeded the call for change—embarking on a quest of discovery.

"I consulted every shaman, every psychic, every priest to learn about what was really important to me what my value system was." The result? "The things that matter most in life are health, family and doing what you love."

Juliet imparts her wisdom to her children, "Do what you love, work hard, tell the truth and be kind."

If only more kindness prevailed at work. Just think what a better place the world would be.

I've said it once, but I'll say it again. Do not, under any circumstances stay in a job that compromises your values, or is making you physically ill. Perhaps, your mindset needs to change. Perhaps it's the job. But whatever the cause, take action now to find the cure.

Conquering stress, this escalating modern day evil is so critical that I devoted a whole chapter to it in my first book, *Mid-Life Career Rescue: The Call For Change*. And readers agree. As one reviewer wrote:

> "I definitely recommend reading the chapter on stress. I wish I had the valuable information she laid out 15 years ago when I went through a 'brown out'—one step before complete burn out.

> If I knew what physical signs to look for I would have left that job way earlier than I did. Unfortunately for me I learned the hard way what a stressful job situation can do to you both mentally and physically, but you don't have to. Instead, you just need to read *Mid-Life Career Rescue*, and follow the advice of Ms. Gaisford."

Tackling stress is so incredibly important that I wrote a whole book dedicated to helping you increase resilience and avoid its toxic reach. *Stress Less. Love Life More: How to Stop Worrying, Reduce Anxiety, Eliminate Negative Thinking and Find Happiness* is available from all good online retailers in an ebook or paperback.

VALUES IN BUSINESS

Organisations have their own values and personalities too. Finding individuals who 'fit' their culture plays a key part in their hiring decisions. And it's a two-way street.

Similarly, your best-fit job or organisation is one that aligns with your values and allows you to be yourself.

Once you have identified your driving values you can begin to look for companies and roles that align with them. For example, if you identified 'passion' as important, look for companies that actively communicate and act upon this value.

Sometimes this may mean doing a little bit of investigative home-work. Don't just rely on what the advertisement or job description says, or what the recruiter or hiring manager tells you. Ask people who work there, customers who deal with them, and even competitors. Get the real story. It's not what they say that counts; it's what they do.

Not all companies actively live and breathe their values. But the truly great companies, businesses and individuals do.

Hot Tip! Increase your chances of a good values match by including a summary of your values in your CV, social media profiles like Linkedin, or your website if you have one.

OVERCOMING VALUES CONFLICTS

The consequences of accepting a role or staying in a job where your values don't 'fit' are huge. Job dissatisfaction; a feeling of not belonging; of not being appreciated, affirmed or valued; and serious depression can occur if no remedial action is taken. These feelings and experiences are commonly referred to as 'values conflicts'.

One of my clients, Lynn, was the editor of a magazine. She had a real gift for innovative and lateral thinking, and creativity was something she valued. She assumed that when she accepted a new position as Chief Editor for another company that her creativity would be something they also valued.

It was a huge shock to learn that they valued maintaining the status quo more than innovation, and that they did not affirm or value the changes she sought to create.

She also valued her independence and autonomy, and in her previous role her boss had been happy for her to work whatever hours and days she liked. His main criteria was that the job got done; he didn't care where or how.

In her new role people preferred to work standard hours and questions were asked and eyebrows were raised when she attempted to work from home or worked anything other than the core Monday to Friday 9am to 5pm hours. Her boss's assumption was, "If I can't see you, you're not working." Not much trust there!

For her own health and happiness, Lynn resigned after three months. She realised that if she stayed any longer it would mean changing the very essence of who she was, and devaluing her needs.

In hindsight, she wished she had taken the time to think about her most important values prior to changing careers, rather than having acted so impulsively.

"I guess I just assumed that it would be similar to where I was before. I could have saved everybody a lot of grief by clarifying my needs and asking a few more questions about the company culture before I started."

ACTION TASK! GET YOUR NEEDS MET

If any of your most important values are not being met to your satisfaction, what changes need to occur so that they are met? Some ways to check if your values are in alignment, and steps you can take to resolve any values conflicts, include:

1) Thinking laterally. Brainstorm with friends all the possible ways that people make a living from each of your main values. Think laterally. The aim is not to make a decision but to build an exhaustive list.

Choosing your best-fit career comes later. Right now, allow yourself to go wild and explore. Who knows what you may find. Use generative, open-ended questions like 'who, where, why, when' to create a wider list. For example, how can I make a living from (insert value)? Who is making a living from (insert value)?

2) Paying attention to your body barometer. Notice the times when you feel inspired—a sure sign your values are aligned. When your values are met there's often a feeling of lightness or calm in your body, or a surge of excitement, joy and elation.

The opposite is also true. Heaviness in your shoulders or heart, a feeling of dread in your chest, a surge of anger through your body, are some of the many ways your body warns you of conflict.

3) Exploring and negotiating. Develop a list of questions designed to confirm whether your values align with any prospective employer or role you are considering. For example, if 'respect' is one of your values you may ask an employer, employee or another stakeholder: "How are differences resolved around here?"

If time freedom is important to you, make sure you negotiate flexible hours as part of your employment package. If work-life balance is important, target companies that actively support this. Check company websites, ask people who work there, or contact organisations like the Equal Employment Opportunities Trust to learn more about who you'd like to work for and why.

4) Asking for your needs to be met. All too often people walk away from perfectly good careers without telling people what they need to feel happy, motivated and productive. "Why is it that people only tell us what they want when they're heading out the door," one frustrated HR manager told me.

'If they valued me, they'd know what I needed," a client once said. Don't rely on people being mind readers, and don't assume they don't care.

I once successfully negotiated working a four-day week in one job, and working from home in another. Initially my request was met with disapproval. I figured they were afraid I wouldn't get my work done, so I suggested we give it a go as a trial.

This allowed them to get comfy with the idea, knowing they could return to the status quo if I didn't deliver. I got heaps more done than being in the office.

If you can't get your needs met, it's time to look elsewhere. I've done this many times in my career.

5) Playtime. If it is not possible at this time to get your needs met in your career, and you're not ready to make a move, pro-actively seek ways to satisfy your values away from work.

Taking up a hobby, joining up with like-minded people or volunteering are just a few possible ways to achieve this. Look for examples of people, places or things that align with your values. Meetup.com is a great place to start.

CLIENT SUCCESS STORY: VALUE IN NEGOTIATING

Janna, a woman in her 50s, had been out of work for several months following the disestablishment of her previous position. She was over the moon when she was interviewed for a position with a company focusing on theatre and performance—an area of personal interest and passion.

However, she was disappointed with the salary being offered, of $45,000 per annum. Her previous role paid $90,000. Her prospective employer was financially constrained and not in a position to offer her more money.

While she was really interested in the role, and money was not a main driver, she was reluctant to take the position, and was seriously considering turning it down.

Sometimes people are too quick to focus on what they think they will be giving up rather than focusing on the things they will be gaining by making a career move.

We worked through a process to look for lateral and creative ways that both parties could get their needs met. Part of this process involved going back and highlighting the things Janna wanted most from her work and life, and all the elements that gave her the most satisfaction.

One of Janna's key motivators was a desire for greater flexibility. She also wanted to spend more time with her children, as well as have time to focus on art and sculpture—things she had previously only had time to do as hobbies. So she was reluctant to step back into a 9 to 5 position.

Together we discussed different strategies that she could suggest to her prospective employer to better sculpt the position to meet her needs, as well as to 'compensate' for the drop in salary.

We also attempted to put a dollar value on these ideas, which included things like negotiating: a four-day week, flexible work arrangements such as working from home, and extended leave of five weeks a year.

These things would not have a direct financial cost to her employer but would give her more wealth in terms of time, flexibility and work-life balance. Plus, the additional benefits of working in a role that she felt passionate about were immeasurable.

The pragmatist in her realised she would still have to earn some additional money to cover some of her expenses and keep the life-style she enjoyed. She was already marketing her art to several New Zealand outlets and, as a result of her networking efforts, she had been offered additional work on terms to suit herself. This career combo and trimming non-essentials from her budget ensured that Janna was able to pursue her dream job and life.

PASSIONATE ANGER

"Put love first. Entertain thoughts that give life And when a thought, or resentment, or hurt, or fear comes your way, have another thought that is more powerful—a thought that is love."

~ Mary Manin Morrissey, Author

"We are what we hate." These lyrics of one of Jack Johnston's songs, provides a powerful reminder about the role of our deepest beliefs and values in defining who we are.

When your values are violated or called into question in some way it's a powerful wake-up call.

The things that stir angry emotions are transparent clues to our values—the deeply held beliefs or rules about what is right or wrong, acceptable or unacceptable.

When used constructively, the things that push your buttons can also provide a powerful clue to work that will make you feel truly fulfilled, and guide you towards your purpose.

HEED THE SIGNS

In the absence of some lightning strike of clarity people often fail to notice the accumulated signs that point them toward their life's work.

As Nelson Mandela said, "There was no particular day on which I said, henceforth I will devote myself to the liberation of my people. Instead, I simply found myself doing so and could not do otherwise.

I had no epiphany, no singular revelation, no moment of truth, but a steady accumulation of a thousand slights, a thousand indignities, and a thousand remembered moments produced in me an anger, a rebelliousness, a desire to fight the system that imprisoned my people."

ACTION QUESTION: WHAT PUSHES YOUR BUTTONS?

As a wise person once said, "The world continues to allow evil because it is not angry enough." What do you hate? What makes you angry? List all the things that push your buttons. How might you use your anger to bring about constructive change?

Empowering Others

Nicki's pet hate was injustice, bullying, and unnecessary intimidation. She created a unique role for herself in the lucrative legal services industry by creating customised legal services that empower people to take control of their issues, strive for mediated solutions, and feel strong and confident in their truth when under attack.

"Our increased life expectancy means people at mid-life can expect another career time that equals the career that's gone before. Only this time it's a career you choose with your eyes open, it's a career that builds on all your experience, that matches your values and passions, that suits the way you like to live and work."

~Fitzsimons and Beckford, Authors

VALUING NATURAL KNACKS AND TALENTS

"If you don't pay attention to what you love, you could overlook your greatest gifts! That love is the sure-fire indicator of hidden gifts, and it is the only way to find them. Skills don't count. They're just abilities that were useful enough to be developed. Gifts often haven't had the chance to be developed and because of that we're fooled into thinking they don't exist."

Barbara Sher, Author

People often think that unless they have received formal training or gained experience on the job, or have a piece of paper like a degree, then they don't have any skills.

This is not true! The world is full of people who have achieved great things without formal training. Sometimes the best course of study is to teach yourself.

How many times have you heard of people who gained a qualification and were then told they lacked practical experience, or that they had to go and unlearn everything an academic institution had taught them?

I'm not knocking formal training. And in some professions, it's essential. But not all career paths require certification, or on the job experience.

No training required!

Van Gogh was a self-taught artist. He used his passion and natural ability with colour and creativity to paint wonderful masterpieces that send hearts racing and are worth millions of dollars today.

From an early age, my brother Hadyn was wheeling and dealing. He has not done an MBA or had any formal training in business. Instead, he uses his natural entrepreneurial skills to create many successful business ventures. He tried going to University but quit because he felt academics were out of touch with reality.

As a child, my daughter Hannah has always had a strong connection to Spirit. Now in her late twenties, she has chosen to her embrace her gifts and has started a career as an intuitive life coach and spiritual medium.

A client of mine trained as a textile designer and, despite a lack of formal training in kitchen design, has successfully combined her passion for beautiful design, and her natural creative ability, into a successful career as an award-winning kitchen designer.

My mother has done the same thing, quitting a job she hated as a legal conveyancer in her 50's, then—after buying into a franchise, she set up her own shop as an interior designer—all with no formal training. A passion for design, a natural talent for creating beauty, a gift for knowing what looks good, and how to market her services, and loving making her clients happy, have seen her become very successful.

Now in her 70's, she's shut her physical store and runs her business from the comfort and beauty of her home. I share more of her story and her practical strategies for building a beautiful business in Mid-Life Career Rescue: Employ Yourself.

THE TRUTH ABOUT SKILLS

"Although men are accused of not knowing their own weaknesses, yet perhaps few know their own strength. It is in men as in soils, where sometimes there is a vein of gold which the owner never knows of." - Jonathon Swift, Satirist

THE COLLINS CONCISE Dictionary defines a skill as "demon-strating accomplishment."

It's that simple. Do what you do well, and communicate your achievements. If you can't do something you love well, up-skill.

There are plenty of ways to do this. Online courses, self-help books, shadowing others—and of course, formal tuition, where needed.

Most often though, there are things you do very, very well. But so many people, mid-lifers, and women especially, tend to undervalue the things that come easily to them.

Three types of skills

The Dictionary of Occupational Titles, a primary text in vocational literature, makes a distinction between three basic types of skills: work-content or technical skills; self-management skills; and functional-transferable skills.

Work content skills: Historically these have been how we've always thought of skills—something in which you have had specific training, or have received a qualification in, rather than a natural ability or life skill.

Whilst technical skills, and specialised knowledge and abilities (often gained through formal education or training) may be important for some occupations, it is essential not to over-inflate their importance.

Many hiring decisions are made on the basis of self-management skills, often referred to as personality traits and preferences. Recruitment firms often use trait-based psychometric assessments tools to determine your aptitude and ability for the job. But they're only one part of the equation, and there's a growing body of research which questions their validity.

Personally and professionally I've always valued preference-based personality assessment tools, and am a certified and qualified practitioner of the Myers Briggs Personality Preference Indicator(MBTI), for this reason.

I'll explain this later in the chapter, but in brief, I rate this tool because it assumes you are the expert in your life, that you know your preferences best, and that if you wish to change—you can. Trait-based tools assume you are what you are, and won't change. They also very often disempower people, by placing others in the role of expert.

Transferable or portable skills: Your self-management skills, along with your natural knacks and talents are the portable skills that are easily transferred into other roles or career paths.

For example, you may have a natural ability for teaching. You may, or may not, have combined this ability with a formal qualification or on the job training. Regardless, this natural skill is highly portable.

Your strongest functional-transferable skills or 'natural knacks" and talents have often been a core theme in your self-expression throughout most of your life.

For example: perhaps as a child, you may have been persuasive with your parents in extending your bedtime; sold the most raffle tickets for your school; talked your friends into joining activities that you wanted to do; and won a debating prize in college. Convincing is a major functional-transferable skill running through these experiences.

The importance of focusing on your functional transferable skills and self-management skills

While ultimately the strongest skills you have in each of these areas must feature in your career planning, it is important to focus on your transferable, portable skills and abilities.

They are the key to entering, redirecting, or changing careers. They are the constant factors you can rely upon to make you marketable, no matter what changes you need or want to make in the types of projects you address or the types of working conditions you have as a context for your work.

Unlike Work Content/Technical Skills, which are role or career, specific, transferable skills may be employed in a wide range of incredibly varied directions.

For example, if you have a natural knack and a passion for organising things, you can market that in a whole host of projects and settings. Some careers that require "organising skills", for example, include: Project Management, Events Management, Administration Support Officer, and Deployment Management, etc.

ACTION TASK! GENERATE IDEAS

Break down the skill of teaching. What is it? Sharing knowledge, passing on skills, something else?

Brainstorm or list all the possible ways people make a living from their skill of teaching. Build your list by using generative thinking skills, and open questions like, 'teach- what, where, why and how?'

If you get stuck do some research. I just entered, "what skills does a teacher have?" into Google and came across some very useful information, including a site devoted to helping people find a new life *after* teaching. The tips they provide are relevant not just to teaching —check it out here >>

To transfer in or out of a career you need to highlight your relevant transferable skills. And, as the link I shared above confirms, action verbs not only do this, they'll make your future job applications, or self-employment branding efforts, 'pop.'

IT'S 'JUST' WHAT YOU DO

People often take their functional-transferable skills for granted because they come so naturally they don't think about them. Often someone's strengths are so much part of who they are and what they do that they don't always realise that what they find easy other people struggle to do. How many times have you been complimented and say, "Oh, it's nothing. It's just what I do."

It's not nothing. Natural talents which, combined with your enthusiasm, create your point of difference. They're pure gold.

As you've read above, Van Gogh had a natural knack for creativity. Hadyn had a natural knack for trading. But the unifying thread, shared by all successful people, is passion.

IT'S YOUR TIME TO SHINE

Many people think that by the time they reach their mid-years knowing what they are good at should be easy. However, as I've highlighted many people tend to take themselves for granted. And an astounding amount of people have suffered from years of neglect and lack of positive feedback.

Combine this with cultural messaging of the past, that work is something to be endured, not enjoyed, makes affirming the positive absolutely vital. As does challenging the notion that it's arrogant to 'blow your own trumpet." How will people know what you're good at if you don't know yourself, and you don't tell anyone?

What gives you joy? What do you love doing? What would you do for free? Answering these questions and noticing the times you feel excited, alive, or in love with doing or being something, are vital signs confirming you are on the path with heart.

Being good at something, without enjoying it, only leads to heartache, boredom, and resentment in the longer term. As one of my unhappy clients said recently, "They keep promoting me but does anyone ever ask me if I like what I do?"

Just like the artists who learn to paint with their feet and their mouths, with the motivation you can learn to master a skill you don't currently have. But without motivation, it can just feel like a painful thing to do.

ACTION TASK! IDENTIFY YOUR FAVOURITE SKILLS AND TALENTS

If you're struggling to identify your favourite skills and natural knacks and talents, the following lists of skills, grouped in related clusters, will help.

This exercise involves three separate stages: rating your joy, ranking your skill and picking the favourite talents you want to use or develop in your career.

1) Do you feel joy, happiness or contentment? When completing this exercise first identify your 'joy factor.' How much enjoyment does using this skill give you? Is it a skill you're motivated to use?

Rate Your Joy Level. Using the skills categories which follow, rate them from 1-5 according to their joy level—1 -low enjoyment and 5 - high enjoyment

This is an important step in finding a job you will love but one so many people ignore. Instead, they concentrate prematurely on how much ability they think they have, forgetting motivation altogether.

2) How skilled are you? Once you have identified your motivation, self-assess your level of skill or competency. Think about your skills in relation to your whole life, not just your work.

Rank your skill Level from A–C. A is a strength, B is you're competent, and C you lack skill. This may be because you've never had the opportunity to use this skill, or because you know it's a weakness or something you need to develop

Don't let your feelings about how much you dislike, or think you would dislike, the activity guide your assessment. A lack of compatibility with your interests, or a clash of values, for example, may be influencing your feelings.

Perhaps you're too hard on yourself. Bring some objectivity to this exercise. Assess your present level of skill by referring to feedback people have given you.

INTERPERSONAL SKILLS

Gaining trust and respect of others/building relationships

Relating to diverse people

Being sensitive to people's needs and feelings/empathy

Building teams

Contributing effectively to teams

Mediating/resolving conflicts/building consensus

Networking/building relationships

Perceiving intuitively (sense, show insight, and foresight)

COMMUNICATION SKILLS

Listening effectively

Writing concisely and persuasively

Speaking persuasively

Translating complex ideas into everyday language

Giving helpful, constructive feedback

Making effective presentations

Having a compelling sales approach/presentation

Speaking to an audience

Interviewing for information

Marketing/selling

Proofreading/editing (checking writing for proper usage and stylistic flair, making improvements)

LEADING/MANAGING SKILLS

Developing and communicating a compelling vision

Inspiring/motivating others/communicating persuasively

Gaining the trust of others

Giving direction/coordinating/organising others

Thinking strategically

Planning

Working effectively under pressure/demanding deadlines

Gaining co-operation of people you have no direct control of

Making decisions

Initiating change (exert influence on changing the status quo, bring about new directions)

DEVELOPING OTHERS/COACHING SKILLS

Counselling, advising

Coaching, training, mentoring and teaching new skills and competencies

Motivating others to achieve their goals

Giving constructive feedback

Mentoring

PLANNING AND ORGANIZING SKILLS

Defining goals and objectives

Prioritising tasks and assignments

Project/event management (schedule and develop projects or programs)

Delegating effectively to make the best use of others' skills

Integrating the efforts of others

Thinking ahead and contingency planning

Coordinating events, handling logistics

Monitoring (keeping track of the movement of data, people or things)

Implementing (providing detailed follow-through or policies or plans)

Expediting (speeding up production or services), troubleshooting problems, streamlining services

Classifying (grouping, categorising, systemising data, people or things)

TIME MANAGEMENT SKILLS

Prioritising to best meet customers'/organisations' needs

Establishing achievable goals and objectives

Balancing work and personal life

Delegating

Prioritizing

LEARNING AND PROFESSIONAL EXPERTISE

Staying current

Developing new skills and knowledge to remain at the top of your game

Being regarded as an expert in your field

Emotional intelligence

Resilience/stress management

FINANCIAL MANAGEMENT/COST SENSITIVITY SKILLS

Preparing budgets, computing costs, etc.

Establishing cost controls

Managing activities to stay within budget

Increasing profitability by reducing overheads

Budgeting, economising, saving, stretching money or other resources

Cash flow forecasting

Taxation

Estimating, appraising, costing

Counting (tallying, calculating, computing quantities)

PROBLEM-SOLVING AND ANALYZING SKILLS

Breaking things down logically

Systematic thinking

Finding facts and information

Researching

Evaluating (assessing, reviewing, critiquing feasibility or quality)

Identifying and diagnosing to get to the root of a problem

Developing innovative, effective solutions to complex problems

CREATIVE SKILLS

Portraying images (sketching, drawing, computer graphics, illustrating, painting, or photographing)

Lateral thinking

Generating ideas (reflecting upon, conceiving, dreaming up, brainstorming, improving)

Composing music (writing and arranging music for instruments or voice)

Entertaining, performing (amusing, singing, dancing, acting, playing music)

Visualising (imagining possibilities, seeing in mind's eye)

Designing (structuring new or innovative processes, programs, products or environments)

Producing skilled crafts

THINKING SKILLS

Seeing the 'big picture'

Conceptualising ideas, models, relationships

Thinking strategically

Integrating and synthesising information from different sources

Forward-thinking—anticipating future needs and requirements

Establishing achievable objectives

Creative/imaginative thinking

RESEARCHING/ANALYZING SKILLS

Initiating projects, interventions, programs

Making decisions and following through

Taking personal responsibility for decisions

Dealing with ambiguity

Gathering information, doing research

Attending to small details

Interpreting underlying themes from complex information

INNOVATION/BUSINESS DEVELOPMENT SKILLS

Identifying and capitalising on opportunities

Developing new products to meet emerging needs

Actively seeking new opportunities

Generating income

CUSTOMER/CLIENT SERVICE SKILLS

Strong customer/client-service focus

Making a real difference to customer/client (high impact)

Building and maintaining relationships

Being seen as a business partner

TECHNICAL SKILLS AND KNOWLEDGE

List any work-specific skills and qualifications you have, i.e., professional qualifications, degrees, technology or machinery, etc. that you can use well.

3) WHAT ARE your favourite skills? Having completed the first two parts of this exercise, you'll have a clear picture of where your joy matches your skill level.

Now list your most motivated skills—both those you are already skilled at and those you would like to develop.

These motivated skills form an important part of your criteria for job satisfaction. You may either chose a role that allows you to work with your strengths or one which helps you develop skills you love but need an opportunity to develop.

This was my strategy when I took a role working for an Employee Assistance Program provider. I turned down other higher paying roles because, although the job paid $30K less, it met my values and my longer-term goal to work for myself.

It was a greenfield role—one that lacked constraints imposed by prior systems and ways of working. It gave me greater freedom and creative control. And I got the chance to develop and grow a business and learn all that entailed, from the safety and security of a salaried position.

My new employer also paid for me to complete my counselling qualification and allowed me time off work to complete the training. Because they already had an established client base, I was also able to build the necessary practical hours to gain my certification.

In addition, skills which once demotivated me, like budgeting and organising, quickly became favourites when I realised how essential mastering them was to be able to develop a successful business.

CLIENT SUCCESS STORY: FROM HOUSEWIFE TO NURSERY MANAGER

Mary had been at home raising her children for 15 years. She was desperate to find paid employment but felt she had no skills and was afraid no one would ever hire her. She felt a skill was something you were trained to do and that you had a piece of paper to prove it.

Career coaching helped her identify that her natural knacks and talents such as planning, researching, writing, planting and cultivating, and creating things were skills and had a commercial value.

"I'd always ignored them and denied I had any ability. They were just something I could do and that came easily to me. Until I saw them as skills I couldn't value them."

Career coaching not only helped Mary gain greater awareness of her strengths but also how they transferred into a wide variety of occupations. She was also able to describe concrete examples of how she has used these skills to accomplish something and to communicate the value of her experience to an employer.

Now, free of self-doubt, she is feeling much more confident about her abilities.

She proactively contacted organisations she would like to work for and after an initial trial period was offered a role as a manager of a local plant centre and nursery.

ACTION TASK! DISCOVER HIDDEN SKILLS

If you'd like further confirmation of your natural knack and talents, or your confidence and self-belief could do with a boost, the following exercises may help.

1) Forage for examples. Gather clippings, articles, job advertisements, and feedback—anything that awakens awareness or reminds you of what you can, or could do well. Notice the times you say, "I could do that!" Surround yourself with images of things that trigger something for you.

2) What comes easily to you? Notice the natural knacks or gifts that are easiest for you. They can provide a good clue to the work-related strengths you are most passionate about.

3) What makes you proud? Looking back over your life, what have been your proudest moments? What skills did you draw upon to make those achievements happen?

4) Collect feedback. Keep a feedback journal or notebook and write down some positive things people have said about you. Drag out any helpful performance reviews. Even your old school reports can confirm areas of core strength. I'll go into this in more depth shortly.

5) Notice clues to passion. Notice the times when you're doing or experiencing something, and you catch yourself saying, "I love..." or you feel excited, alive or inspired. Write them down so you don't forget them. Add to this, "I could get more of this feeling by..."

Many people find it difficult to give examples of how they have used their skills—after all, we don't go around analysing ourselves, and our actions on a daily basis. Collecting positive feedback that others have said about you provides an objective way to record and confirm your skills, passions, and areas of strength.

The best-selling author of *What Color is Your Parachute*, Richard Bolles, believes, as I do, that we are unable to truly realise our strengths without the insight provided by others.

Collecting feedback makes it possible to recognise and affirm strengths that you may have overlooked or discounted.

The power of collecting feedback is powerfully summed up by businesswoman, Barbara Koziarski, in Kay Douglas' book, *Living Out Loud: 22 Inspiring New Zealand Women Share their Wisdom.*

> *"I realised that I had been collecting evidence of failures, telling myself 'I can't do this because...' and sometimes they were old failure messages from the past.*

"To overcome my doubts and fears I started to look for and collect evidence of my success… sometimes people would come up to me and say, 'You really spoke to me. That touched me,' and I'd go home and write that down.

"So I started to think that I was worthwhile because I had proof of it. And once I could shore myself up with the external proof I got better at not needing it."

You may wish to keep your feedback in an inspirational feedback journal so that you can refer to it often throughout the career transition process. Include feedback you've received in the past by thinking back over your lifetime, from childhood through to the present, and recalling insights into your strengths that people have expressed to you.

Sources of feedback could include family, friends, clients, employers, co-workers, old school reports, performance reviews, thank you cards and emails, etc. Don't forget to update your feedback journal regularly.

You may only hear the 'negative feedback' and catch the volley of criticisms sometimes lobbed at you - so looking for, and recording, instances of positive feedback is a great counter strategy.

SURF THE NET

I've been keeping feedback in a special journal for years. Like Barbara, I'm a lot more believing of my abilities now and don't update it as regularly as I once did. But whenever I need a motivational boost, it's a nice book to read. Click the following link to see one of my older journals. (http://bit.ly/2zoHCKH)

GETTING BELOW THE SURFACE—WHAT EMPLOYERS REALLY WANT

You can teach someone new skills with minimum effort. The challenge comes when you try to change somebody's natural inclination.

Many employers are more concerned with "softer skills" and attributes that are less easily taught. Your chances of succeeding during a career transition are greater when you list and give examples of your passions, motives, interests, values, personality traits and attributes. The stuff beneath the tip of the iceberg!

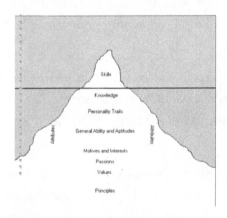

Do What You Are. How Personality Profiling Can Help

Personality tools and psychological assessment can really help in the quest to determine what you want to do and where you want to be when it comes to transitioning into a new career or rekindling the passion for the role you currently have.

Based on the premise of 'doing what you are,' good quality assessment tools can help people gain more objective insight into their key strengths and talents, values and motivators. Knowing what is under the bonnet makes it much easier to fine-tune your high

74

performance engine, and therefore navigate yourself in the direction that best energises you.

The more you know about yourself the better your decisions will be and the more chance you will have of presenting yourself and your natural talent in the best light to employers.

There are many personality assessment tools around. One of the most popular is the Myers Briggs Type Indicator (MBTI). This is a world-renowned and powerful personality inventory used extensively to help people develop greater awareness of both their own personalities and those they live or work with.

The MBTI was developed in the United States by a mother-and-daughter team, Katherine Briggs and Isabel Myers. The Indicator is based on the work of Swiss psychologist Carl Jung.

It simplifies what can be a very complex area and provides a useful, easy to understand method and language for understanding people. By looking at eight personality preferences that everyone uses at different times you will learn more about how to get the best from yourself and also others.

These preferences influence behaviour and are divided into four areas:

1. How people get and use their energy—through interaction with the world or inner reflection (extraversion or introversion)
2. How people gather and take in information – a preference for factual, concrete information or ideas, theories and future visioning (sensing or intuition)
3. Make decisions—through a logical 'head' process or a personalised 'heart' process (thinking or feeling)
4. Organise their lives—in a planned, organised, scheduled

way or in a flexible, open, spontaneous way (judging or perceiving).

While we all use each of these parts of our personality, just like we use both our right and left hands, according to MBTI theory, people prefer one of each pair over the other and will instinctively operate in this way unless they are consciously working with their non-preferred preferences.

For example, if you prefer being planned and organised it is less likely that you will be comfortable going with the flow and 'winging it' unless you are consciously making an effort. These instinctive, innate ways of being can provide clues to your natural knacks and talents.

I like the MBTI as an assessment tool because it is not trait-based, and use it often with clients. It does not assume some fixed, immovable quality – with motivation you are free to change. And in this openness to change you can master a new skill, a new way of being. A new life. A new point of brilliance.

I often refer to the calendars produced by artists who paint with their mouths and their feet. They weren't born with a natural talent for painting this way, but having lost the use of their hands or arms, and motivated to express themselves, they focused their efforts on acquiring new mastery.

It's easier and much better to work with your strengths. But, as you will read later in this chapter, your weaknesses, if left unattended can derail you, preventing you from realising the success and happiness you might otherwise have achieved.

When I wanted to become more detail-focused (typically associated with Sensing), I thought of friends for whom this is a strength, and who I admire, and said to myself, before tackling a task 'what would Christine and Laurie do now?"

The answer came quickly. "Read slowly, read with fresh eyes, pause before sending emails, and allow more time—less haste, more perfection."

I've done the same with the qualities I've wanted to develop, like patience. "What would Mother Theresa do now?" She wouldn't shout! She wouldn't lose her cool. She'd send loving and kindness and smile.

Right now in my writing career, I want to better balance my preference for generating ideas, and variety—evidenced by focusing on many, many projects and not always finishing things in a timely manner—with completion.

These qualities are typically associated with 'N" or Intuition, combined with "Perceiving." I think of an authorpreneur I admire, Joanna Penn (a confessed "J") and I think what would Joanna do now? I know she's very good at saying 'no' to requests on her time and energy that don't further her goals. That's great, healthy self and professional care. Something I'm learning to do more of – personally and professionally.

Neuropsychologist, Katherine Benziger says, "People are happiest, healthiest and most effective when developing, using and being rewarded for using their natural gifts."

This is very true. But it's also incredibly fulfilling nurturing your Achilles heel and mastering new skills and abilities. If we keep doing what we've always done we'll always get what we've always got, right?

ACTION TASK! WHAT MAKES YOU TICK?

If you know your preferences, perhaps because you've completed the questionnaire through work, dust off your report and list all your ingredients of career satisfaction, strengths and areas for development.

Trawl through the Internet and Google types of careers pursued by people with similar preferences to you.

If you've never completed the MBTI, the questionnaire can be completed via the Internet and takes only 20–30 minutes to complete. Once you have completed it, the results will be compiled into an extensive report.

This report is an invaluable personal and professional development tool, which provides insights into your personality preferences, including:

• Characteristics of your personality type

• Strengths and weaknesses

• Natural gifts and talents

• Careers and work environments suited to your personality type

• Blind spots and areas for development

• Communication preferences and relationship management skills

• How other people see you

• How you react under pressure and stress

• Conflict management.

Only you know yourself best, and unlike other personality tools the MBTI is not considered an accurate assessment of your personality until you have had the opportunity to confirm and verify that the results have accurately 'captured' your personality.

This feedback session can occur in several ways including, face-to-face coaching sessions, email and Skype coaching, and during career and/or life coaching discussions.

Personality tests and 'types' aren't cast in granite, but are a useful way of increasing your self-awareness about how you naturally and instinctively tend to think and work. You can then build on that base to help you with your ongoing professional and personal development.

A word of caution, for accurate results, be sure to complete the authorised questionnaire, available only from qualified profession-als, like me. Take a look at the sample and see how detailed the report is: http://www.cpp.com/images/reports/smp267149.pdf

"TAP into and have confidence in the things that come easily to you. Your natural knacks provide clues to your talents, values, passion, purpose, and potential. They are uniquely you, make you happy, and give you the edge."

~Laurie Wills, Change-maker

CLIENT SUCCESS STORY: CLARIFYING PERSONALITY LEADS TO DREAM CAREER

Sanjay, a man in his 50s had been made redundant from a senior science management role. The loss of his job was a big shock and severely damaged his pride, self-esteem, and confidence. When he first came to me for help he asked, "Do you think I have any skills?"

I was astounded. This man was seriously skilled, with an amazing track record of achievement. But I also know how crippling redundancy can be to people's confidence.

Clarifying his personality preferences helped Sanjay rediscover and value his unique strengths and natural talents. By pinpointing the things that energised him, and gave him life, personality profiling also helped him market himself into a new job.

As an ESFJ, Sanjay's formula for career satisfaction included large amounts of face-to-face interaction with people, an environment where he could maintain warm and genuine interpersonal relationships with other people and a role which involved working in a real and tangible way to improve the quality of people's lives.

It was also important to him to be able to organise and control his work and those around him so that things ran as smoothly and efficiently as possible. Combining all these elements with his interests in problem-solving, science and a life-long dream of owning his own business one day, Sanjay successfully secured a role as the CEO of a nationally based advisory group.

"The outcome for me from Cassandra's program was a renewed passion and belief in myself, a clear understanding of my strengths and direction on areas that I wish to improve to assist me with my future goals."

One of the strategies I encouraged him to do was to shine the spotlight on what we both agreed the selection panel may have regarded as his weakness of flaw.

"You're probably thinking, what can a 55-year-old Indian man from South Africa with no experience in the building industry, bring to the role," he challenged.

Then, with confidence, he answered his own question by emphasising how his weaknesses were strengths. Including, the ability to stand back and see things with fresh eyes and a track record of leading transformational change, etc.

Not only did Sanjay get a top job—he beat other people who had more industry experience.

FAITH IN THE STARS—ASTROLOGY FOR CAREER CHANGE AND SELF- AWARENESS

"I liked the idea that astrology believes we all are special and have unique gifts. It was at that moment that my love of astrology was born." ~ Marianne O'Hagan, Astrologer

So many people put their faith in psychometric tests, many of which are resounding failures in predicting job satisfaction, happiness or superior performance. Why not put your faith in the stars?

"Personality testing used in job interviews was the cause of much of my self-doubt and lack of belief in my skills and abilities," Pauline, a counsellor, shared with me recently. And I know others have felt the same.

Whether you're a believer or a non-believer, taking a peek at your astrological profile can boost awareness, confirm areas of potential strength, fuel belief and instils confidence.

Many years ago, bogged down by family dramas and workplace stress I sought the help of Marianne O'Hagan, a very accomplished, but also a very science-based astrologer. I was blown away by how much she knew about me.

I later wrote what became a very popular article for the business and careers section of the New Zealand Herald, '*An astrologist uses mathematics to predict success.*'

For convenience and inspiration, I've included it below. Are you a skeptic? Great. So was I. Are you open-minded? Good, then give it a try.

From Comptometer Operator to Astrologer

Despite having endured more than her fair share of suffering, Marianne O'Hagan is a woman who exudes warmth, compassion and a zest for life. Her traumatic childhood experiences, deep love of humanity and multiple job losses have guided Marianne to her true purpose in life. She has carved out an impressive niche for herself as an astrologist.

> "My twin sister and I were born into poverty during an air raid in south London at the time of the Second World War. Unlike my sister, I was born with clubfeet. My mother's first words, 'Oh what a shame', plagued me for years where I felt constantly ashamed for not being a 'normal' child," she says.
>
> Lengthy, frequent and painful trips to the specialist to correct her feet meant she missed much of her schooling. On top of this, an accident that left her deaf in one ear meant that for most of her childhood she was told she was stupid.
>
> Naturally left-handed, raps on the hand designed to "encourage" her to use her right hand further hindered her ability to communicate.
>
> Born under the sign of Taurus, Marianne dug her heels in and fought her way to success. She caught up on her schooling and mastered the ability to walk. But the trauma of her childhood scarred her self-esteem.
>
> Marianne clearly remembers the day, during a period of deep questioning, that astrology became her life's purpose.

"Mother was reading her daily horoscope. I asked her what it meant, and she told me that everyone had a star sign and that mine was Taurus the Bull. I suddenly realised that I was the same as everyone else - we all had star signs and we all belonged. I felt a deep sense of knowing. I liked the idea that astrology believes we all are special and have unique gifts. It was at that moment that my love of astrology was born."

Marianne read voraciously on the subject; she coupled her reading with her love of mathematics and natural ability with numbers and soon began drawing up astrology charts for her friends. She had an uncanny ability to predict people's behaviour and forecast how their patterns and planetary activity influenced their lives.

Marianne's passion for astrology remained a hobby for many years while she pursued more traditional careers. Initially, she started her career as a hairdresser. Although she loved it she couldn't stand on her feet all day and after six months reluctantly had to give it up.

"At that time I thought, what do I want to do with my life? I knew I loved maths so I set my sights on being a comptometer operator (the first commercially successful key-driven mechanical calculator). In those days it was a pretty prestigious job. I targeted a company who used these things, started at the bottom and was offered the opportunity to train.

"At first, I was shocked. All my life I'd been told I was stupid and wouldn't amount to anything and then my boss offered me the chance to train in an area I'd dreamed of. I cried."

Later she up-skilled as an accountant. She was good at the work but missed contact with people. While doing a stint as a recruitment agent she met a New Zealander, who she later married. They moved to New Zealand where she secured a top job working in a chartered accountancy. Two years later the company folded. She soon found another role but several years later she was made redundant again. As the economy worsened, work became less secure and Marianne faced six redundancies over a 15-year period. "I decided God was telling me it was time to start my own business," she recalls.

Instead of taking the easy option and setting up her on her own as an accountant, she decided to choose the path with heart and follow her passion for astrology.

"I changed my name, changed my vocation and my life changed. I made more money than I ever did working for someone else and I've helped so many people," she says.

Doors quickly opened. She was asked to run seminars, which were hugely successful, and was then approached by Radio 2ZB. During the following three years she popularised astrology through radio talk back and became Wellington's leading astrological consultant. With over 34 years' experience, she now attracts clients from all over the world.

Several years ago, a near-death experience following a cerebral haemorrhage gave Marianne a new lease on life and she focused her efforts on writing her first astrology book, Lunar Astrology from the Horses Mouth, which she says will revolutionise the way people look at astrology.

"We all know how the moon affects the tides. Drawing the water in or releasing it out. If we are 90 per cent fluid it makes sense that humans are affected by the planets too," Marianne says.

"I began by applying the phases of the moon to people and characterising people born under the various phrases. After seven years of research, and hundreds of interviews I saw how accurate lunar astrology was. People really did respond to that phase."

So just how can astrology help?

"Most clients come with financial problems or relationship problems," Marianne says. "They come looking for the hope of happiness in the future."

According to Marianne, predicting success in others is all based on mathematics. "It's the mathematical positions of the planets that actually create events - as simple as the tides going out at high tide, twice a day, and it's predictable."

She asks people for the time and place of birth prior to meeting them and draws up their astrological chart so she can understand, and, in turn, help them to understand, the aspects influencing them.

As a result of their personalised astrological consultation, clients who have come to Marianne under extremely difficult circumstances leave with a deeper understanding of themselves, their problems and how to solve them.

"All my life I prayed to God, 'God please make me a normal child like all the other kids'. But I see now that all this time I was being groomed for my life purpose. I have tremendous empathy for people and a deep compassion. People come to me for readings but what I am really doing is counselling them. I love helping people."

SURF THE NET

In her late-70's, at the time of writing, Marianne is still living and working with passion. You can watch a short interview we did together on YouTube here: https://youtu.be/IuCrlnAyD4w

Lunar Astrology from the Horses Mouth is available from Marianne O'Hagan's website: www.marianneohagan.com. You'll also find her contact details there if you wish to book an astrology session in person, via phone or Skype.

"Love is not only something you feel.
It's something you do."
David Wilkerson, founding pastor of Times Square Church, New York City

WHAT YOU'VE LEARNED SO FAR

- Passion flows, it can't be forced. Don't underestimate the things that come easiest to you. Your natural knacks, talents, and gifts often reveal your true path with heart.
- The world of work is full of numerous examples of people who have succeeded despite a lack of formal training.
- Your natural knacks, talents and hidden gifts can reveal

your unique source of difference. They're the skills and abilities that come most easily to you and mixed with motivation and interest lead to your unique PassionPoint and point of brilliance.

- Skills can be categorized into three areas—work and industry-specific, non-transferable skills; self-management or personality traits and preferences; and transferable skills.
- Emphasizing your portable skills and how these readily transfer into different occupations and industries will give you the edge when changing careers.
- Increased self-awareness brings added objectivity and clarity to the career planning process.
- Assessing and increasing your awareness of the range of skills, talents and gifts you have, can be achieved in a variety of ways including, both conventional methods—such as self-assessment, third-party feedback, and personality profiling - and less 'conventional', more spiritual approaches, including astrology and other techniques which help you remember, affirm and value your authentic self.

WHAT'S NEXT?

If work is getting you down, or your self-belief could do with a boost, the last chapter will increase your awareness of simple and effective ways to create transformational change.

"You know when you have a skill you've got to go out there and share it. You know if you look at a phenomenal dancer, an incredible athlete, a wonderful musician, you think wow, 'that's a human being and they can do that.' And it makes you feel good about human beings."
Marisa Peer, Celebrity Hypnotherapist and Author

III

STRATEGIES TO BOOST HAPPINESS AT WORK

RE-ENGINEER YOUR CURRENT JOB

"I propose a radical, yet ancient notion: To build the life you want—complete with inner satisfaction, personal meaning and rewards – create the work you love."

Marsha Sinetar, Author

You don't always need to quit your current line of work to experience more happiness. As Laurie's story below highlights, sometimes you just have to re-engineer where, how and when you do your work. Energy goes, where energy flows. If you're not thriving, identify your stressors and make a change for the better.

FROM CHAINED TO THE OFFICE, TO FREEDOM IN THE COUNTRY

"What counts for me, in business and in life, is making a difference. That and having fun. Okay, it's not always fun. Sometimes it's b***** stressful," says Laurie Wills, a mortgage expert with a passion for butterflies.

"But work feels less like a slog when I get to help awesome people make their dreams come true. I'm lucky to have clients I'm proud to call friends. Of course the odd bottle of champers I'm sometimes sent, goes down a treat too."

But Laurie yearned to be free from the confines of an office. He wondered if he just needed a break from the industry. But then after analysing what he really needed to be happier at work, it came down to two central themes. More freedom and control.

He sold his shares in the first mortgage business, and after a short break, started a new business, *Awesome Mortgages*. With a vision for the future and a blue-print about how he wanted to operate, he re-engineered his processes. An early adopter of new technology, he remains, at the time of writing, one of the first mortgages advisors working remotely in New Zealand.

"It was exciting to see some of my clients make a move to a warmer climate, and I thought, 'that's what I want to do too."

It was an audacious move that definitely paid off. Together with his partner, they left Wellington, and moved onto their own lifestyle block, overlooking the magical Bay of Islands, near Kerikeri.

It was a dream that wouldn't have come, had he not spent time early on in his career planning, getting clarity about how he wanted to live and work in the future. But the move wasn't without some apprehension.

"How will people feel if we're based in the Winterless North," I wondered. "Will they balk and walk if they can't do business over a caffeine shot? What about the tie, the dark suit, the polished shoes? Will a T-shirt and shorts send the wrong message?

"I thought it could, but my partner, said, 'Trust me. It's what you do, the results you get, and the integrity you do it with, that attracts people to you, and keeps them coming back. That, and all those razor-sharp deals.'

"We kept our dreams alive, by creating a manifestation board on the fridge. One of the captions we pasted was, 'Thriving Up North'. And that vision has come true. This financial year has been the biggest, most financially successful in my career as a mortgage expert. I'm on track to have helped my clients purchase in excess of $65 million dollars worth of property. And best of all, we're both happier as a couple, and I've still been able to pursue my passions.

Laurie's passion is researching exotic butterflies. He is renown by many as the Indiana Jones of the butterfly world, due to his exploits and intrepid exploring in jungles, inaccessible mountains, and dangerous landscapes. He's discovered many new species new to science and co-authored several important scientific articles.

His passion sustains him, but he accepts, it's not something he can make the kind of living he aspires too. While he's also passionate about negotiating the best outcomes for his home-buying clients, his day-job funds his lifestyle and passion. And now that he's taken control back and re-engineered where, when and how he does his work, he has better balance.

"Some of the negotiations I've concluded while up a tree, butterfly net in one hand, iPhone in the other, while in Papua New Guinea. I've also helped people to buy homes while I've been high in the mountains of war-torn Bougainville.

"Then there were the mortgage negotiations made all the sweeter while I was swinging in a hammock in Fiji. But most of my help has been given while enjoying my own slice of paradise back home. I really do think the warmer climate has given me superpowers when it comes to getting the best outcomes for my clients."

Yip, there's a myth in the mortgage industry, Laurie has happily proved wrong, that you have to don a tie, work relentless nights and weekends, and invade peoples' privacy by going to their homes.

By making positive changes in his life, changes that better reflect how he wants to live and work, he's proved recent research conducted by the University of Cologne right. Happier people earn more money.

At the time of writing, he's just headed away for a week of R&R with his son Nick, who's just finished the 6th form at Wellington College. It will be father and son bonding—which he says, makes working hard even sweeter.

FIND YOUR HAPPY PLACE TO WORK

Being happier at work can involve something as simple but as transformative as changing your environment. Many mid-lifers find they are more productive, more prosperous, more delighted and inspired when they change where they work.

When I was deep into the final edits for this book, 1 thought I'd head to one of my happy places to work. Straight away I thought of Wharepuke, my local award-winning restaurant, and cafe, surrounded by tropical gardens.

Although I am also happy working from my home overlooking the sea, sometimes it's lovely being surrounded by happy people. I'm sure you'll feel this energy in the book. Working independently of an office was a cherished dream I've happily made true.

I know another lady, who dreams of working under her lemon tree. And others who live their dreams, by working in funky open-plan offices, surrounded by heaps of cool people. Many people dream of working in the sanctuary of their home, or while traveling the world.

So many things are possible. Only you can take yourself where you need to go. If you're trapped in a cubicle, or deep in the dungeons of a grotty prison, as I once was, even a poster or screen saver can transport you far-far away.

ACTION QUESTION: WHERE'S YOUR HAPPY PLACE

Where's your favourite place to work?

If you don't like your current space, what steps can you take to improve your working environment?

SURF THE NET

Watch my impromptu video, and gain some tips about creating your place of happiness click here >>http://vimeo.com/148318116

"Until you know that life is interesting—and find it so—you haven't found your soul."
Archbishop Geoffrey Fisher

SHIFT INGRAINED BELIEFS

"You've got to believe in what you're doing. You can't stay in the void of self-doubt. It's holding you back. It's like a bike—you've got to let go of the training wheels and say, "I can do this. I can do this without the training wheels."

Laurie Wills

Does the quote above say something to you? It did to me. That was my partner giving me a motivational blast, back in March (2015).

My previous lack of confidence surprised so many people who know me. I've always adopted the 'fake it 'till you make it' policy when needed. But self-doubt had always held me back from tackling some of the bigger projects I yearned to do.

I've been reasonably confident at things I didn't enjoy as much, or where there seemed to be less at stake. But I've been less believing when it came to following passions that seemed so beyond my capability. Like writing a historical art-related novel, something I once thought was beyond my realm of competence and am currently tackling.

"You can't make a living from something you love," a woman told one of my coaches, recently. I hear that all the time. You might have too. Or, maybe deep down, there's a persistent voice telling you, you're not good enough, or you can't have what you want.

But what if the opposite were true? What if making a living from what you love is exactly what you can do.

It's the messages you tell yourself that matter most, says celebrity Hypnotherapist and Author Marisa Peers. "Belief without talent will get you further than talent with no belief. If you have the two you will be unstoppable."

Chances are you don't need to see a therapist to move beyond self-limiting beliefs, but if you do, great. Go do it. There's magic in that.

You can also learn from some of the most powerful, effective and simple techniques used by practitioners working in the realm of positive psychology and mind reprogramming.

"When our strategies are simple and solution-oriented, we can develop effective and compelling futures," says the founder of Solution-Focused Brief Therapy, Inso Kim Berg.

The questions below, drawn both from Solution-Focused techniques, and Cognitive Behavioural Therapy (CBT), could help you challenge your fears and move forward courageously.

ACTION QUESTIONS: CHALLENGE YOUR BELIEFS

Acknowledge the things you don't believe and challenge them. Interview your beliefs, by asking them the following questions.

"Where's your evidence for that?" (That being whatever you fear or hold to be true?)

"What's the worse that could happen if you pursued your passion? How bad would that really be? How can you increase the likelihood of success?"

"What tells you that you could follow your dreams?" (a nice shift from focusing on the problem to looking for solutions instead.)

"What have you tried recently that worked? What you are you doing now that works?"

"Who do you know who is happy at work? What could you learn from them?"

"How does your (supportive other) know you can do this? What difference will it make to them when you are happier?"

Interestingly, the woman I mentioned above, having responded to this challenge, returned to her next session, bubbling with happiness. "You'll never believe it. Someone asked if I would do their make-up for them and they offered to pay me!"

Believe it! When you let desire, not fear propel you forward, magic happens. It's the Law of Attraction. The Law of Manifestation. The Law of Intention. But it only works if you stay positive. Negativity is a repellent. Positivity is a magnet, drawing abundance forward.

SHIFTING INGRAINED BELIEFS

So often we aren't even aware of what our self-limiting beliefs are. If your beliefs are ingrained, or you keep sabotaging your own success, seeking help from a qualified practitioner with expertise in reprogramming stubborn, disempowering beliefs may be a game-changer.

I did this recently, when once again synchronicity struck. A wonderful counsellor I was training to be a life coach recommended the book, *The Biology of Belief: Unleashing the Power of Consciousness, Matter & Miracles,* by Bruce Lipton. Bruce is an American developmental biologist best known for promoting the idea that genes and DNA can be manipulated by a person's beliefs.

In his book, he shares how he experienced a paradigm shift while at a conference. "I told my audience that if they changed their *beliefs* they could change their lives. It was a familiar conclusion with familiar responses from participants: 'Well Bruce, that's great, but how do we do that?'"

Back then Bruce, like so many of us, didn't fully realise the crucial role the subconscious mind plays in the change process. "Instead, I relied mostly on trying to power through negative behaviour using positive thinking and willpower. I knew, though, that I had had only limited success in making personal changes in my own life.

I also knew that when I offered this solution, the energy in the room dropped like a lead balloon. It seems my sophisticated audiences had already tried willpower and positive thinking with limited success."

Fate intervened, for Bruce as it did for me when I was guided to his book. So often life whispers to us, but we fail to tune in. In Bruce's case, the messenger he needed to hear was sitting right next to him, psychotherapist Rob Williams, the Creator of PSYCH-K, who was presenting at the same conference.

"Rob's opening remarks quickly had the entire audience on the edge of our seats. In his introduction, Rob stated that PSYCH-K can change long-standing, limiting beliefs in a matter of minutes."

In Bruce's book, *The Biology of Belief,* he shares how, in less than 10 minutes, a woman paralysed by her fear of public speaking, transformed into a confident, excited and visibly relaxed person up on the stage. The transformation he witnessed was astounding. So much so that Bruce has used PYSCH-K in his own life.

I thought, "I'd love to give that a try." I was intrigued, as Bruce was, but skeptical too. Why not be open to something that could fast-track my success, I decided. Bruce Lipton is no lightweight, no beaded, hippy guru, but a credentialed, highly acclaimed and respected man in the world of science. I trusted him.

But I believed it would be impossible to find someone trained in this technique in my new home, the small township of Kerikeri, in the Far North of New Zealand.

I was proved wrong! See how our beliefs can fool us? Anyhow, long story, short, my sore foot demanded attention first and led me to Jane Bromley, a reflexologist. To my great delight, Jane was also a highly skilled practitioner of PSYCH-K.

To find out more about the fabulous Jane Bromley you'll find her here: www.janebromley.com. At the time of writing, her new website was under construction.

Looking back I think my sore foot was a message from Spirit telling me it was time to stand on my own two feet again, to reclaim my authentic self, and pursue my independence as an author speaking her own truth. Authenticity. This is key to my empowered change, as I know it will be for you. Follow your own truth, as I have done in the past, and am super-charging now. It will set you free.

"PSYCH-K has helped me undo my self-limiting beliefs, including one about not being able to finish my book," Bruce wrote at the end of his book.

That struck a chord with me. I felt a trill of excitement. Not a thrill, but a trill—a song deep in my heart. Bruce was like the pied piper and I was happy to follow. I had so many unfinished books, including (at the time) this one.

But now, you're reading my second book. And a month after finishing this one I released my third, *Midlife Career Rescue: Employ Yourself*, followed quickly by a fourth, *How to Find Your Passion and Purpose*. All my books have been finished and published within four weeks, and all achieved #1 bestseller on Amazon as soon as they were released—with five-star reviews too!

PSYCH-K, and other books and self-empowerment tools, I've leveraged off over the years, have helped me clear out the debris and wounds of the past—endured in this life and those prior. I'm grateful for all that I am and all that I was, and I'm excited about the future SELF I'm recreating.

I have a sense of excitement for you. Oh, the places you shall go!

Believe in what you do and who you are

WHAT YOU'VE LEARNED SO FAR

- You don't always need to quit your current line of work to experience more happiness.
- To build the life you want—satisfying, personal meaningful and rewarding – change anything that is not working and recreate the work you love.

- Happier people earn more money, have more fulfilling relationships and enjoy better health and quality of life.
- Being happier at work can involve something as simple as changing your environment.
- It's the messages you tell yourself that matter most. It's easier to succeed when talent is *combined* with belief.
- If your self-belief could do with a boost, learn from experts in positive psychology and mind reprogramming. Go deeper to shift ingrained beliefs by tapping into the realms where science meets spirituality.

WHAT'S NEXT?

You've heard the call, you know what brings you joy, contentment and bliss. You've found your capabilities, your aspirations, your longings, and your hidden talents. You've found your passion and you know what makes you happy.

You've got all you need to know to embark on new experiences and to make life-affirming choices. You have all the seeds to plant new beginnings. You may feel a knot in your gut as you prepare to make a leap, but you're excited.

You are on a new path, about to embark on a new life-changing journey. You are being offered a blank page to rescript the new story of your life—what are the first words you'd like to write?

Your possibilities are infinite. You are empowered and in complete control of your life. Have a foot in the future but stay grounded in the present. Have faith and trust in yourself and your abilities. Plant the seeds of your aspirations, nurture and protect them, and watch them grow into the prosperous fruits of your passion.

Do you have the courage? Do you have the courage of your convictions to bring forth this work? The treasures that are living inside you are hoping you will say 'yes!'

You're empowered with a checklist to aid decision-making. This will take the stress out of worrying you'll make the wrong move, and super-charge the confidence needed to make an inspired change.

Take a leap of faith and venture forth. Live out loud and go for your dream.

Are you ready to quit your job? Try the following Ready to Quit Quiz to see how many of these 'quitting signs' are true for you.

THE READY TO QUIT QUIZ

- You find it hard to get out of bed in the morning.
- You're often late for work.
- Once you arrive at work, it takes you a while to actually get started working.
- You sit at your desk and daydream.
- You have less patience with customers or co-workers than you used to.
- You spend time at work doing personal tasks.
- You look at job websites on the Internet when you're at work.
- You get impatient with rules and red tape on the job.
- You take longer breaks then you should.
- When you have to phone people as part of your job you spend more time chatting than you need to.
- You feel tired during the workday.
- You don't bother mentioning concerns to the boss or HR because it's usually a waste of time.
- If you leave the office during the day, you take your time getting back to work.

- You do the minimum amount of work required.
- You check the time throughout the day to see how close to quitting time it is.
- You feel bored at work.
- You 'kill time' during the day by chatting with co-workers or doing other non-essential tasks.
- You schedule medical and other personal appointments during working hours.
- You start getting ready to leave work before knock off time.
- You're out the door as soon as it's quitting time.
- You spend a lot of time complaining about what's not going right at work.
- On the weekends you look at the job classifieds or surf job websites
- You've called in sick when you could've worked.
- You complain about your job.
- You have trouble sleeping on Sunday nights because you're thinking about having to go back to work.
- When you're on holidays you dread going back to work.

Scoring:

If you answered "yes" to more than six but less than 14 of these statements, you are moderately dis-satisfied. While you're not ready to quit, you could benefit from getting clearer about what makes you happy at work. Then you may be able to take steps to change things for the better. If not, it may be time to quit.

. . .

IF YOU ANSWERED "YES" to 14 but less than 20 of these statements you have a great level of dis-satisfaction with your current job. If you can't improve things for the better, it may be time to make a move.

IF YOU ANSWERED "YES" 20 of these statements - why are you still working there? It's time to identify career options that you will enjoy and be successful at.

YOUR POINT OF BRILLIANCE

YOUR POINT OF BRILLIANCE

Your point of brilliance is where you truly shine. It's your point of passion. It's the intersection of your favourite gifts, and talents, your deepest interests, and enthusiasms, and all that motivates, inspires, and drives you.

It's the place of fire and alchemy, magnetising and attracting people, situations and opportunities to you.

But you must show up. You must commit to being authentically you. And you must stand in your own truth. You know what makes you bloom and what makes you wither. You know when you're opening and when you're closing.

Be deliberate and focused in the pursuit of your happiness. Target your intentions on your dreams and desires, and ensure your choices align with what makes you happy.

Get real about your motives. Why do you want to reach your goals? Are your following your path with heart, your life purpose, your true destiny? If you follow a chosen path, will you reach your place of true bliss and authentic happiness?

Are you grounded in your truth, or are you chasing someone else's goals or the lure of fantasy and ego?

Remember the perfect career for you is one that:

✓ You're passionate about

✓ Interests you

✓ Fills you with purpose

✓ Aligns with your highest values

✓ Utilises your favourite talents

✓ Allows you to express yourself

✓ Fulfils your potential

✓ Facilitates your growth

✓ Feeds your mind, body, and soul

✓ Boosts self-esteem and confidence

✓ Makes you happy

✓ Fuels your energy

✓ Gives life

✓ Enables your goals

✓ Is your point of brilliance

They're not unrealistic expectations. Target your intentions, and shoot straight for the stars. Don't settle for anything less, unless you have a compelling reason why.

It's easy to lose your focus, and forget what's really important. You may be offered a shiny new role, only to find, too late, it doesn't meet your needs.

Evaluating Career Options

When evaluating a career choice there are four possible things that can happen:

1) A job can look right—but isn't. This is dangerous. So many people launch themselves into new roles only to find the job wasn't all it was cracked up to be. Having committed to a change people often find it hard to walk away.

2) A job can look right and is. Perfect—it's the right job for you and you don't need to worry about making a mistake or fret that a better job may be out there.

3) A job can look wrong and it is. Once again this is a good outcome because you won't allow self-doubt and indecision to confuse you. Similarly, you won't allow other people to talk you into taking a job that isn't your best-fit career.

4) A job can look wrong and it isn't. Prematurely judging a job and deciding it's not for them is where many people go wrong. Sometimes well-meaning family and friends can steer you away from your best-fit career. Or perhaps you've made untested assumptions about what this role or industry is really like.

When I went into recruitment I really had no idea that so much of the job was about sales. I worked in a very individualist culture where making a commission was more important than helping people find careers and work environments suited to their strengths and aspirations. Working like this nearly killed me. Only after I got shingles did I gain the strength to leave. This was a classic, 'A job can look right—but isn't.'

My next job ended up being the perfect job for me, but I very nearly turned it down. Moving from an international consultancy to a not-for-profit was quite a change. People accused me of taking a backward step and warned that I was "going to the brown cardigan brigade."

At the same time, I was offered another role that paid $30k more. But my heart wasn't in it. My rational mind tried to talk me into it —on paper, the higher-paying role looked way better. But intuitively I knew my best-fit career was working for a values-based company whose mission in life was to help others.

Strategically I also knew the lower-paying role was going to advance my salary prospects by helping me gain experience in the things I lacked. Evaluating the options against my checklist of career fulfilment helped me make the right decision—a whole-brained one that honoured my heart and my intellect.

Keeping my eye firmly fixed on my goals has also helped me make short-term sacrifices. Sometimes this has meant sucking in my pride and starting at the bottom. Or taking a pay cut to get the leverage I needed.

You may find it helpful to summarise the insights you've gained from reading *Mid-Life Career Rescue* in your Passion Journal. The following exercise can also be a lifesaver.

Action Task! Summarise Your Criteria for Happiness

Creating your checklist for authentic happiness will help you stay on track, and provide a handy tool to evaluate current and future opportunities.

If you're a list-maker, create a list. If you're more creative, draw, paint, or collage your criteria for life and work fulfilment.

Your Passion Point is your Point of Brilliance

I've always loved John Ruskin's quote, "Where talent, interest, and motivation intersect expect a masterpiece."

Using this as your guide, you may like to draw three circles. List your areas of motivation in one (passion, purpose, values, goals etc); Your interests and obsessions in another; Your favourite skills and talents in the third.

Note where they overlap. This is your internal world, and what I call your PassionPoint, or Point of Brilliance. Your PassionPoint is your sweet spot.

Surround these three circles with a fourth to enclose them. This symbolises the external world—both the practical earth and the higher heavens.

Action Question: How Can Your Point Of Brilliance Serve?

To generate career options, knowing what will be needed or in demand, now and in the future, can yield gold. What needs can you fulfil when you're aligned with your PassionPoint? What economic, demographic, social, environmental or other needs can you serve? This is the work you are called to do and where you will truly shine.

It doesn't need to have a fancy job title or be about saving the world. But whatever you chose to do has to fulfil a need. Economics 101—no need, no demand. Of course, if money is no barrier, you are freer to pursue your own needs without this added focus. By doing this you may just create a demand, or make the world a happier place. Importantly, you'll be happy.

Hot Tip! Always, always evaluate job and career choices against your non-negotiable criteria for happiness. Don't settle. This is the time to go for your highest intentions. Be clear that you're pointing in the right direction. Don't be seduced by quick, 'get it now' ideas.

Balance The Law of Intention with The Law of Detachment

Remember to balance the Law of Intention with The Law of Detachment. Nothing you want is upstream. Resist the urge to panic, if things don't happen as quickly as you'd like. Go with the flow. Trust. Cultivate Faith. Believe. Allow no doubt.

You may think the outcome has to happen in a certain way, on a certain day, to reach your goal. But human willpower can't make everything happen. Spirit has its own idea, of how the arrow flies, and upon what wind it travels.

It may not happen overnight, but if you maintain your focus, and take inspired action, and follow your heart, your time will come.

I promise!

If by some strange twist of fate, it doesn't? As Annie Featherston shared in the first chapter, "Even if I had never succeeded I would have known that at least I tried."

A life of no regrets - now that's worth striving for.

"My mother said to me, 'If you are a soldier, you will become a general. If you are a monk you will become the Pope.' Instead, I was a painter, and became Picasso."

~ Pablo Picasso, Artist

THE READY TO QUIT QUIZZ

IS IT TIME TO QUIT YOUR JOB? LOOK FOR THE TELL-TALE SIGNS

Most people who want to quit their jobs behave in ways that are noticeably different from employees who are happy at work.

Try the following Ready to Quit Quiz to see how many of these 'quitting signs' are true for you.

THE READY TO QUIT QUIZ

1. You find it hard to get out of bed in the morning.

2. You're often late for work.

3. Once you arrive at work, it takes you a while to actually get started working.

4. You sit at your desk and daydream.

5. You have less patience with customers or co-workers than you used to.

6. You spend time at work doing personal tasks.

7. You look at job websites on the Internet when you're at work.

8. You get impatient with rules and red tape on the job.

9. You take longer breaks then you should.

10. When you have to phone people as part of your job you spend more time chatting than you need to.

11. You feel tired during the workday.

12. You don't bother mentioning concerns to the boss or HR because it's usually a waste of time.

13. If you leave the office during the day, you take your time getting back to work.

14. You do the minimum amount of work required.

15. You check the time throughout the day to see how close to quitting time it is.

16. You feel bored at work.

17. You 'kill time' during the day by chatting with co-workers or doing other non-essential tasks.

18. You schedule medical and other personal appointments during working hours.

19. You start getting ready to leave work before knock off time.

20. You're out the door as soon as it's quitting time.

21. You spend a lot of time complaining about what's not going right at work.

22. On the weekends you look at the job classifieds or surf job websites

23. You've called in sick when you could've worked.

24. You complain about your job.

25. You have trouble sleeping on Sunday nights because you're thinking about having to go back to work.

26. When you're on holidays you dread going back to work.

SCORING:

If you answered "yes" to more than six but less than 14 of these statements, you are moderately dis-satisfied. While you're not ready to quit, you could benefit from getting clearer about what makes you happy at work. Then you may be able to take steps to change things for the better. If not, it may be time to quit.

If you answered "yes" to 14 but less than 20 of these statements you have a great level of dissatisfaction with your current job. If you can't improve things for the better, it may be time to make a move.

If you answered "yes" 20 of these statements—why are you still working there? It's time to make a move to a job you love!

AFTERWORD

Mid-Life Career Rescue has given me the confidence, the security, the faith, the power of belief, and the validation that following your passion is the only way to live.

I feel freer, less burdened, less caring, in an empowered way, of what people think or feel. I write what I believe. I write what I feel. I write what I want to read. And I write to help myself.

If my words inspire you, if my words make a difference, if my words empower you to make a change for the better, then I am happy. Thrilled. Elated. But it will not have been because of me - it will have been because of you.

You are the one who has changed. I will have had the privilege of providing a spark, a light, a beam to shine along your sacred path. But you will have taken the route less traveled. If not now, soon :)

Thank you for trusting me to guide you. I really hope you loved this book as much as I loved writing it. And I hope it aids your growth, as I have grown and flourished as I wrote.

Please keep in touch. Write to me, if you feel like it, and let me know how you're doing. I promise to write back.

In gratitude and with love,

Cassandra

P.S. If you're still teetering on the edge of change, don't worry. That's normal. Everything in good time. But take comfort if you're not yet in the right frame of mind.

It's hard to feel inspired, impossible to be creative, and challenging to feel confident, if you're stressed out of your mind, believe you've left it too late to change, or are trapped by narrow thinking

Pick up a copy *Mid-Life Career Rescue: The call for change* and use it as your guide. If you already have it, revisit it again. It may just give you the extra oomph you need.

P.P.S. BE IN THE KNOW!

If you'd like to be the first to know when other books become available, sign up for my newsletter and receive free giveaways, sneak peeks into new books and helpful tips and strategies to live life more passionately.

** FREE BONUS **

Are you considering the freedom of becoming your own boss? Read to the end for free chapters from *Employ Yourself*, the third book in the Career-Rescue Series.

FREE WORKBOOK!

The Passion Journal: The Effortless Path to Manifesting Your Love, Life, and Career Goals

Thank you for your interest in my new book.
To show my appreciation, I'm excited to be giving you another book for FREE!

Download the free *Passion Journal Workbook* here>>https://dl.bookfunnel.com/aepj97k2n1

I hope you enjoy it—it's dedicated to helping you live and work with passion, resilience and joy.

You'll also be subscribed to my newsletter and receive free give-aways, insights into my writing life, new release advance alerts and inspirational tips to help you live and work with passion, joy, and prosperity. Opt out at anytime.

ALSO BY CASSANDRA GAISFORD

Transformational Super Kids:

The Little Princess
The Little Princess Can Fly
I Have to Grow
The Boy Who Cried
Jojo Lost Her Confidence
Lulu is a Black Sheep
Why Doesn't Mummy Love Me?

Mid-Life Career Rescue:

The Call for Change
What Makes You Happy
Employ Yourself
Job Search Strategies That Work
3 Book Box Set: The Call for Change, What Makes You Happy, Employ Yourself

4 Book Box Set: The Call for Change, What Makes You Happy, Employ Yourself, Job Search Strategies That Work

Career Change:

Career Change 2020 5 Book-Bundle Box Set

Master Life Coach:

Leonardo da Vinci: Life Coach
Coco Chanel: Life Coach

The Art of Living:

How to Find Your Passion and Purpose
How to Find Your Passion and Purpose Companion Workbook
Career Rescue: The Art and Science of Reinventing Your Career and Life
Boost Your Self-Esteem and Confidence
Anxiety Rescue
No! Why 'No' is the New 'Yes'
How to Find Your Joy and Purpose
How to Find Your Joy and Purpose Companion Workbook

The Art of Success:

Leonardo da Vinci
Coco Chanel

Journaling Prompts Series:

The Passion Journal
The Passion-Driven Business Planning Journal

How to Find Your Passion and Purpose 2 Book-Bundle Box Set

Health & Happiness:

The Happy, Healthy Artist
Stress Less. Love Life More
Bounce: Overcoming Adversity, Building Resilience and Finding Joy
Bounce Companion Workbook

Mindful Sobriety:

Mind Your Drink: The Surprising Joy of Sobriety
Mind Over Mojitos: How Moderating Your Drinking Can Change Your Life: Easy Recipes for Happier Hours & a Joy-Filled Life
Your Beautiful Brain: Control Alcohol and Love Life More

Happy Sobriety:

Happy Sobriety: Non-Alcoholic Guilt-Free Drinks You'll Love
The Sobriety Journal
Happy Sobriety Two Book Bundle-Box Set: Alcohol and Guilt-Free Drinks You'll Love & *The Sobriety Journal*

Money Manifestation:

Financial Rescue: The Total Money Makeover: Create Wealth, Reduce Debt & Gain Freedom

The Prosperous Author:

Developing a Millionaire Mindset
Productivity Hacks: Do Less & Make More
Two Book Bundle-Box Set (Books 1-2)

Miracle Mindset:

Change Your Mindset: Millionaire Mindset Makeover: The Power of Purpose, Passion, & Perseverance

Non-Fiction:

Where is Salvator Mundi?

More of Cassandra's practical and inspiring workbooks on a range of career and life-enhancing topics are on her website (www.cassandragaisford.com) and her author page at all good online bookstores.

NOW IN AUDIO!

Did you know you can enjoy and be inspired by Cassandra's most popular and successful books on audio? In less than 15 minutes you could be listening your way to a new life!

Check out the following written and narrated by Cassandra:

Mid-Life Career Rescue: The Career For Change

How to Find Your Passion and Purpose

How to Find Your Joy and Purpose

The Little Princess

The Little Princess Can Fly

I Have to Grow

The Boy Who Cried

AUDIO VERSIONS OF THESE AND OTHER TITLES
AVAILABLE NOW FROM ALL ONLINE BOOKSTORES
AND LIBRARIES.

NEW RELEASES

Word By Word:Lessons on Writing, Love, and Life
Think Outside The Box: How to Change Careers with Creative
Thinking

FOLLOW YOUR PASSION TO PROSPERITY ONLINE COURSE

If you need more help to find and live your life purpose you may prefer to take my online course. Watch inspirational and practical videos and other strategies to help you to fulfill your potential.

Follow your passion and purpose to prosperity—online coaching program

Easily discover your passion and purpose, overcoming barriers to success, and create a job or business you love with my self-paced online course.

Gain unlimited lifetime access to this course, for as long as you like —across any and all devices you own. Be supported by me and gain practical, inspirational, easy-to-access strategies to achieve your dreams.

To start achieving outstanding personal and professional results with absolute certainty and excitement. **Click here to enroll or find out more—the-coaching-lab.teachable.com/p/follow-your-passion-and-purpose-to-prosperity**

FURTHER RESOURCES

SURF THE NET

www.aarp.org/work—information and tools to help you stay current, connected and connected with what's hot and what's not in today's workplace.

www.entrepreneur.com/howto—your go to place for all the latest tips and strategies from leading experts

www.gettingthingsdone.com—the official home of the work-life management system that has helped countless individuals and organisations bring order to chaos.

www.venusclubs.co.nz—a business community designed to help women in business thrive.

www.lifereimagined.org—loads of inspiration and practical tips to help you maximise your interests and expertise, personalised and interactive.

www.whatthebleep.com—a powerful and inspiring site emphasising quantum physics and the transformational power of thought.

www.heartmath.org—comprehensive information and tools to help you access your intuitive insight and heart based knowledge. Validated and supported by science-based research.

www.personalitytype.com—owned by the authors of *Do What You Are: Discover the Perfect Career for You through the Secrets of Personality Type*—this site focuses on expanding your awareness of your own type and that of others—including children and partners. This site also contains many useful links.

Join polymath Tim Ferris and learn from his interesting and informative guests on The Tim Ferris Show http://fourhourworkweek.com/podcast/

www.eeotrust.co.nz – contains a variety of articles about issues related to mature workers.

www.thirdage.com—contains a variety of holistic articles and online classes designed to help mid-lifers get the most from their lives.

www.careers.govt.nz—a comprehensive site funded by The NZ government to help you make career decisions. research jobs and salaries, find out about training, and access free resources.

www.careerjet.co.nz—an employment search engine allowing you to access thousands of jobs globally.

www.seek.co.nz —sign up for job alerts or search their current vacancies.

www.jobs.govt.nz—you'll find a wide range of Government jobs on this site.

www.monster.com - go global on this website. Search for international or local positions and access a wide range of career related resources.

BOOKS—BUSINESS/PERSONAL SUCCESS

I read a book once. It changed my life. The ones below did too:

Retire Young, Retire Rich

Robert Kiyosaki; http://amzn.to/1P8r5bg

The 4-Hour Work Week: Escape the 9-5, Live Anywhere and Join the New Rich

Tim Ferris; *http://amzn.to/1P8nNok*

Think and Grow Rich

Napoleon Hill; *http://amzn.to/1nyW0Xc*

The Work We Were Born to Do

Nick Williams; http://amzn.to/1nyWQmL

The Business You Were Born to Create

Nick Williams; *http://amzn.to/1nyXkZU*

Trust Your Gut: How the Power of Intuition Can Grow Your Business

Lynn Robinson; http://amzn.to/1nyYJ2Q

Richard Branson: *Losing My Virginity: How I Survived, Had Fun, and Made A Fortune*

The 7 Habits of Highly Effective People

Stephen Covey; *http://amzn.to/1nyZjgO*

The Worrywart's Companion: Twenty-One Ways to Soothe Yourself and Worry Smart

Beverly A. Potter; http://amzn.to/1nyZVDc

Lovemarks: The Future Beyond Brands

Kevin Roberts, *http://amzn.to/1Kl3uaD*

Brain-Ding The Strategy: A Successful Marketing Plan Has to Include BRAIN-DING As The Ultimate Strategy

Francisco J. Serrano, http://amzn.to/1m7UMB6

Dream Big (Olivia)

Ian Falconer; http://amzn.to/1PsIS0D

It's Not How Good You Are, It's How Good You Want to Be

Paul Arden; http://amzn.to/1Kl4iwi

Steal Like an Artist

Austin Kleon; *http://amzn.to/1JWS90s*

Show Your Work

Austin Kleon; *http://amzn.to/1o4mm3N*

The Spontaneous Fulfillment of Desire: Harnessing the Infinite Power of Coincidence

Deepak Chopra; *http://amzn.to/1meW1hW*

The Biology of Belief: Unleashing the Power of Consciousness, Matter & Miracles

Bruce Lipton; *http://amzn.to/1nQGXJ8*

StandOut 2.0: Assess Your Strengths, Find Your Edge, Win at Work

Marcus Buckingham; http://amzn.to/20PMrl9

Thrive: The Third Metric to Redefining Success and Creating a Happier Life

Arianna Huffington; http://amzn.to/1KJEmum

ABOUT THE AUTHOR

CASSANDRA GAISFORD is best known as *The Queen of Uplifting Inspiration.*

She is a holistic therapist, award-winning artist, and #1 bestselling author. A corporate escapee, she now lives and works from her idyllic lifestyle property overlooking the Bay of Islands in New Zealand.

Cassandra's unique blend of business experience and qualifications (BCA, Dip Psych.), creative skills, and wellness and holistic training (Dip Counselling, Reiki Master Teacher) blends pragmatism and commercial savvy with rare and unique insight and out-of-the-box-thinking for anyone wanting to achieve an extraordinary life.

PLEASE LEAVE A REVIEW

Word of mouth is the most powerful marketing force in the universe. If you found this book useful, I'd appreciate you rating this book and leaving a review. You don't have to say much—just a few words about how the book helped you learn something new or made you feel.

"Your books are a fantastic resource and until now I never even thought to write a review. Going forward I will be reviewing more books. So many great ones out there and I want to support the amazing people that write them."

Great reviews help people find good books.

Thank you so much! I appreciate you!

PS: If you enjoyed this book, do me a small favor to help spread the word about it and share on Facebook, Twitter and other social networks.

STAY IN TOUCH

Become a fan and Continue To Be Supported, Encouraged, and Inspired

Subscribe to my newsletter and follow me on BookBub (https://www.bookbub.com/profile/cassandra-gaisford) and be the first to know about my new releases and giveaways

www.cassandragaisford.com
www.facebook.com/powerfulcreativity
www.instagram.com/cassandragaisford
www.youtube.com/cassandragaisfordnz
www.pinterest.com/cassandraNZ
www.linkedin.com/in/cassandragaisford
www.twitter.com/cassandraNZ

BLOG

Subscribe and be inspired by regular posts to help you increase your wellness, follow your bliss, slay self-doubt, and sustain healthy habits.

Learn more about how to achieve happiness and success at work and life by visiting my blog:

www.cassandragaisford.com/archives

SPEAKING EVENTS

Cassandra is available internationally for speaking events aimed at wellness strategies, motivation, inspiration and as a keynote speaker.

She has an enthusiastic, humorous and passionate style of delivery and is celebrated for her ability to motivate, inspire and enlighten.

For information navigate to www.cassandragaisford.com/contact/speaking

To ask Cassandra to come and speak at your workplace or conference, contact: cassandra@cassandragaisford.com

NEWSLETTERS

For inspiring tools and helpful tips subscribe to Cassandra's free newsletters here:
http://www.cassandragaisford.com

Sign up now and receive a free eBook to help you find your passion and purpose!
http://eepurl.com/bEArfT

ACKNOWLEDGMENTS

This book (and my new life) was made possible by the amazing generosity, open-heartedness and wonderful friendship of so many people. Thank you!

To all the amazing, interesting clients who have allowed me to help them over the years, and to the wonderful people who read my newspaper columns and wrote to me with their stories of reinvention—thank you. Your feedback, deep sharing, requests for help and inspired, courageous action, continues to inspire me.

And to the love of my life—Lorenzo, my Templar Knight. Thank you for putting up with all the late nights I spent writing. But mostly, thank you for loving me.

And to you dear reader. Thank you for reading my books and for allowing me to play a small part in your beautiful future. Here's to an extraordinary level of happiness and contentment in all our lives.

With love

COPYRIGHT

intended as a substitute for psychotherapy, counselling, or consulting with your physician.

The intent of the author is only to offer information of a general nature to help you in your quest for emotional, physical, and spiritual well-being.

Any use of information in this book is at the reader's discretion and risk. Neither the author nor the publisher can be held responsible for any loss, claim or damage arising out of the use, or misuse, of the suggestions made, the failure to take medical advice or for any material on third party websites.

ISBN PRINT: 978-0-9941314-1-6

ISBN EBOOK: 978-0-9951250-4-9

ISBN HARDCOVER: 978-1-99-002002-5

Third Edition

EXCERPT: MID-LIFE CAREER RESCUE (EMPLOY YOURSELF)

CHOOSE AND GROW YOUR OWN BUSINESS WITH CONFIDENCE

You don't always need buckets of money, or the courage of a lion, to start your own business. Plenty of successful entrepreneurs have started their businesses on a shoe-string budget and launched new careers while combining salaried employment. Many have felt the fear and launched their business anyway.

I was in my mid-30's, a single parent, holding down a steady job, when I started my first business, Worklife Solutions. I was worried and fearful that I'd fail, but I did it anyway. It's one of the most creative, joyful endeavours I've ever done.

Since then I've created many more businesses and helped people all over the globe become successfully self-employed. Like some of the people who share their stories in this book, and other budding entrepreneurs who've taken a strategic route to finance their businesses.

When I first started out in business over a decade ago, I thought about all the people I knew, or had read about, that were successful in their own business. What I found then, still applies today. The list below is what they have in common. As you read this list think how many strategies could apply to you:

They were doing something they love; their passion drove them.

Making money was not their sole motivation. Their businesses grew from a desire to serve others; they were not trying to force something on others or to make a killer sale. Instead, they wanted to make a positive difference and create something of value. They didn't badger people into buying their goods or service.

1. **They cared about whether or not they could help a prospective client.** If they could, great. If not, they were either quietly persistent until they were needed, or they moved on.
2. **They planned for success.** Their business and marketing plans were living documents and they managed their finances extraordinarily well.
3. **They shared.** They communicated their vision, goals and plans with those important to them, and they researched their clients and stakeholders constantly to learn how to do things better *together*.
4. **They listened.** They listened to their staff, their families

and their clients. Then, and only then, when they understood their issues, fears, needs and desires did they offer a solution.

5. **They started smart.** When employing others, whether on contract or as salaried staff, they hired the right people for the right job, and employed people who were strong in areas they were not. When skill gaps appeared, they gave their people the training, systems, environment and recognition to do their job well.

6. **They took calculated risks.** They always looked before they leapt, but they leapt nonetheless. Courage and confidence was something they built as they went.

7. **They believed in themselves, or faked it!** Even professionals doubt themselves–but they don't let self-doubt win.

"YOU HAVE to believe in yourself. Even when you don't, you have to try," encourages Serena Williams, tennis super-star and 23-time Grand Slam champion.

"There are moments when I am on the court and I'm like, 'I don't think I'm going to be able to do this'. But then I fortify myself and say, 'I can, I can'–and it happens. If you believe in yourself, even if other people don't, that really permeates through and it shows. And people respect that."

IF THE STRATEGIES above sound like things you can do, or are willing to try, chances are self-employment is right for you. But to double check, try the following Entrepreneurial Personality Quiz.

THE ENTREPRENEURIAL PERSONALITY QUIZ

Do you have the right personality to be an entrepreneur? Are you better suited to becoming a Franchisee? Would contracting suit you better? Or is paid employment really the best option after all?

Before committing yourself to starting your own business of any type, you need to ask yourself whether you have what it takes.

The following quiz is written as though you are still in a salaried role. If you have already started your own business, respond to the questions as though you are still in your last job. Answer as you really are, not how you would like to be.

1. Is accomplishing something meaningful with your life important to you?
2. Do you typically set both short and long-term goals for yourself?
3. Do you usually achieve your goals?
4. Do you enjoy working on your own?
5. Do you like to perform a variety of tasks in your job?
6. Are you self-disciplined?

7. Do you like to be in control of your working environment?

8. Do you take full responsibility for your successes and failures?

9. Are you in excellent physical, mental, and emotional health?

10. Do you have the drive and energy to achieve your goals?

11. Do you have work experience in the type of business you wish to start?

12. Have you ever been so engrossed in your work that time passed unnoticed?

13. Do you consider 'failures' as opportunities to learn and grow?

14. Can you hold to your ideas and goals even when others disagree with you?

15. Are you willing to take moderate risks to achieve your goals?

16. Can you afford to lose the money you invest in your business?

17. When the need arises, are you willing to do a job that may not interest you?

18. Are you willing to work hard to acquire new skills?

19. Do you usually stick with a project until it is completed?

20. Does your family support and stand by you in everything you do?

21. Are you organised and methodical in your work?

22. Does it frustrate you when you can't buy the things you want?

23. Do you like taking calculated gambles?

24. Would you still want your own business, even if there were plenty of other good jobs?

25. Are you a people person?

26. Do you handle personal finances well?

27. As an employee did you/do you regularly suggest new ideas at various levels?
28. Do you feel that you can truly shape your own destiny?
29. How flexible are you when approaching work tasks? If things become difficult do you adapt and complete the task?
30. Is the money you could make one of the primary reasons for starting your own business?

Scoring:

Your answers to at least 20 of these questions should be yes if you are to be successful as a business owner.

The more 'yes' answers, the more likely you are to enjoy the entrepreneurial life and be successful as a business owner.

It is not necessary to answer yes to each of these questions, but if you answer no to some of them you will want to evaluate what that means to you and how significantly it may impact your ability to run your own business.

SUCCESS STORY: A FORK IN
THE ROAD

Sheree Clark followed her enthusiasm—her passion for helping others and sharing what she had learned through her own life challenges led her to start her coaching business.

The seeds of change were also cultivated during a stressful time in her life and her former job. She shares her journey of mid-life career reinvention below:

> "My current business is Fork in the Road. I am a healthy living (life) coach. I chose the name initially because I was focused on food and healthful eating, and since "fork" conjures up the idea of eating, it seemed to fit. I also believe that at any given point we are all at a proverbial fork in the road.
>
> That fork can be a major one—such as a career choice or the decision to enter or leave a marriage—or a small one, like whether to say yes to dessert or being on another committee. So, when the focus of my business shifted to life

coaching for women over 40, the name was still (and perhaps even more) fitting for my practice.

Fork in the Road is truly a crescendo of all of my life experience. I work with my clients to transform their health, reclaim vitality and mental focus, and help ensure they gain clarity on their vision and purpose. These are all things I have done for myself over the course of the last 6+ decades of life.

Deciding what to do

My first business was a marketing communications (advertising) agency that I was "talked into" co-founding in 1985 by a (then) new boyfriend. The truth is, I had grown bored at my job at a local university and had even announced my resignation, effective the following academic year (long notices are an accepted practice at US academic institutions). In the meantime, I had met—and fallen in love with—my later-to-be business partner, and the rest fell into place.

He convinced me that my skill set as a teacher, advisor and mentor would transfer easily to the business development aspect of running an advertising agency. We stayed business partners for 25 years (although the romantic aspect tanked after the initial 14 years).

My current business began after I decided to leave the agency world and (my now-ex) behind.

During my time owning the agency, I had taken a variety of classes simply out of an interest in personal development. Many of the courses had to do with health, nutrition and emotional maturity.

Eventually, as I became less interested in the marketing work and more involved in the business of human potential, it became harder to rally enthusiasm for owning an agency.

Finally, just as we were preparing to commemorate 25 years in business together, I told my partner I wanted to exit our partnership to begin something new.

At that point, I still wasn't certain what my new work would look like, but I knew it wasn't fair to anyone (most especially me!) to stay where I knew I was no longer fully engaged.

So, in essence, I quit—and then I figured it out.

Finding an idea that would be successful—ask your way to success

I found the right product for the right market by trial and error! Next to creating a vision board, the informational interview is my favourite tool for helping me get back on track when I'm feeling lost.

When I was feeling unfulfilled in my business I scheduled a series of interviews with fellow entrepreneurs. I picked women who owned businesses. The only thing they had in common was that I really respected them, even though some I had never met in person.

One of my interviews was with the publisher of a local business newspaper: a fabulous lady who is probably 20 years my senior. We had our meeting over lunch and I told her, candidly, about my inner feelings. I told her I was hoping she might shed some light.

I asked her what she thought my skill sets and offerings were and where I might be able to plug the gaps. Her feedback? She said she had always thought of me as a teacher and a coach. She said she saw me as articulate, smart and capable, (which in itself is nice to hear, especially coming from someone you admire).

And then she offered up a casual suggestion. She said, "You've always had a way with words. Why don't you write a column for a publication in your industry or some area of your life that brings you joy." Well, that was an idea that resonated, and if nothing else was worth seeing if I could make happen.

The payoff

I went back to my office and sent a query letter to the editor of a graphic design magazine I had written for once or twice before, and asked if they were looking for writers.

Within an hour my phone rang. It was the editor himself. His words nearly knocked me off my chair. He said, "Wow, what timing! We are starting a business advice column in the next quarter, wanna write it?"

I ended up writing that column for five years. Not only did it help scratch an itch I was feeling, I made some extra money in the process. Now, I am not saying you'll have such epic results. But I do know that I have never had an informational interview without a payoff, even if it was just that I got to know somebody a little better.

Working your offerings into your own area of genius

It's not just about finding the right products and services, it's also about working your offerings into your own area of genius.

At this point in my life, while I enjoy making a good income, it's not only about maximising revenue. I want to do work that brings me joy. I want to work with clients who are a fit for me, so that when I look at my calendar/schedule, I feel excitement, rather than dread.

In my instance, I am what we call a "Baby Boomer" (defined in the USA as being those born between 1946 and 1965). My generation and those slightly after, are all experiencing some major life challenges right now. Our jobs are changing or we've been laid off or deemed "redundant."

Our marriages and family structures are shifting or crumbling: we may suddenly become caretakers or divorcees or widows. Hell, our own bodies are changing and often it feels as though they are betraying us. And for many women over 40, after putting the needs of others first for much of our lives, we can finally say, "it's MY turn now."

What I just described is my area of genius. It's the arena I do best in and it's where I feel most at home. Having for the most part successfully navigated the challenges of being a 40, 50, 60-year old, I get to share my secrets and techniques with other women.

Starting fresh—financing a new career

In both cases when I started my companies I left what I had been doing to embark on the new thing. In the first instance (co-founding the agency) I felt safe doing so because I had a partner and so my risk/exposure was shared.

In the second instance (becoming a coach), I had the luxury of having built savings from the first endeavour, so I could plunge into the second. I recognise that not everyone will have such good fortune.

In both cases, I didn't need any start-up capital.

If I were to give advice, I'd say that while of course you have to consider your own financial situation, also take stock of your risk tolerance.

Entrepreneurship is not certain. There are all sorts of risks and no guarantees. If a lack of financial uncertainty makes you nervous, it's certainly safer to ease into being a business owner, but it can also be more challenging. There are only so many hours in a day!

Finding the confidence to leave the security of a regular salary

It wasn't confidence that propelled me into my second business. It was the pain of not living authentically.

It would be an understatement to say that to close the ad agency I had co-founded was not a decision my former partner and I made easily or lightly. For almost half our lives we had been partners and close friends. But the time had come and we each wanted to do other things with our lives.

I had found a passion in the health and nutrition arena after receiving my certifications as a raw vegan chef and nutrition counsellor.

My business partner discovered a love of fine art, and a desire to work more independently. Quite frankly, we both had become rather miserable in our roles as principals and we each needed new challenges.

Despite my excitement for my new future I struggled to dismantle what we had so carefully created. At the time, we decided to close the agency, it was still healthy but my partner's and my passions were on life support.

There were many signs that it was time for a change. I started to dread the out of town travel for clients that I had once so loved. He began to come into the office later and leave earlier.

We both had less patience for employee mistakes and client indecision. For me the defining moment came on a Sunday at church when I actually cried not because the sermon was so moving, but because I knew that in less than 24 hours I had to "go back to work."

It was clearly time to do something.

There are those who have applauded both of us for having the courage to do something so drastic, and others who deem us insane when we could be 'so close to retirement.' All I know is that, as scary as it was, it has rekindled the adrenalin rushes I have not felt in a very, very long time. It was absolutely the right thing to do.

Finding customers

My clients typically follow me online for a period of time before contracting with me for services. Often they run across me because I am a guest speaker at live events, or a subject matter expert on television, or a guest on an online interview series or summit. Others may have been referred to me by a friend or a colleague.

The marketing activities which have been most important and successful for me are speaking and interviews. I also write guest blogs and articles.

Maintaining balance

Running a business should not be a 24/7 thing! Although there are absolutely "push" times, especially in the beginning, I think down time and rest are essential to business success

Down time, time to refuel, is made possible by setting priorities, delegation and hiring (or subcontracting) efficiently. I personally find balance by planning my days the night before.

Each night before I go to bed, I establish what the most important project or priority is for the next day, and that project is the first thing I address after I do my exercise and meditation.

I also find that sometimes I have to actually schedule in my fun times. With my current work schedule, I coach clients the first three weeks of the month.

The last week of every month I take off from individual coaching, and that is when I attend to personal matters such as doing errands, scheduling salon services and meeting friends for social engagements.

I still do work during that fourth week, but because I don't typically schedule client appointments, I have time for other things.

Keeping energy levels high

It's not hard to have high energy when you have high enthusiasm. I love what I do and it keeps me young, vital, engaged and energised. That said, taking care of yourself mentally emotionally and spiritually is also critical. I get adequate sleep, exercise and nutrition. I spend time in nature and in contemplation or prayer.

I have deep relationships. AND I have a coach. That may sound odd, because I AM a coach, but I believe those of us who are most successful, have gotten where we're at with help in identifying blocks, challenges and opportunities. That is what a coach does!

The secret to success, managing cash flow, and generating regular income

For me personally, I have always benefitted from finding and utilising a good business coach and what is often called a 'mastermind community.' A mastermind is a group of like-minded people who meet regularly to share strategies and tackle challenges and problems together. They lean on each other, give advice, share connections and do business with each other when appropriate.

It's very much peer-to-peer mentoring, and it works! In terms of managing cash flow: one piece of advice is to not take your foot off the 'new business development' gas pedal when you get busy with other things. What you do today will determine your level of success tomorrow.

The learning curve

The biggest learning curve I had was going from owning a company that sold its services in a business to business arena (the communications agency) to one that provided services via a business to consumer model (my coaching practice).

These two ways of conducting business are drastically different. Again, by seeking guidance from peers and by hiring a coach I was able to manage the amount of growing pain.

The best times in my business have usually been the "firsts." First client, first employee, first million-dollar year. The worst have usually been the result of going against my own intuition. Hiring someone I had a gut feeling about because they looked good on paper. Taking a poorly calculated risk because I was listening to my ego instead of looking at the facts or my intuition.

One of the best business books I have read is, *Turning Pro* by Steven Pressfield. It applies to everyone, but entrepreneurs especially.

What advice would you give to someone who has never started a business or been self-employed?

Start by taking the time to meet with other entrepreneurs and ask them a few questions about things that may have you concerned or sparked your curiosity.

This book, *Mid-Life Career Rescue: Employ Yourself,* is a great start, because it gives you a general 'peek under the tent' at being a business owner, but I would also speak to others in real time.

I often urge my clients to schedule what I refer as an 'informational interview' when they are considering going down new paths or are feeling stuck in some area of their lives.

What are the steps to self-employment? Is there a "right" order?

I have taken the leap to self-employment twice, and each time was different from the other. I think there are too many factors to make a generalised bit of advice valuable here. One caveat I would say to the analytical readers is "don't overthink it."

With my current business, I began by sending a letter to everyone I knew from my former business, telling them what I was transitioning to, and straight-out asking them if they might be interested in my services, or if they would be willing to make a referral. I had enough takers to be encouraged to keep going!

Making the leap sooner

I would have left my first company to start my second company sooner. I was afraid of letting people down: my former partner, my employees, my clients. By the time I left, my passion was on life support.

If I could offer one piece of advice related to starting your own business and employing yourself it would be to know that being an entrepreneur can be lonely sometimes. Your friends, the ones who are employed by others, will think you have it made now.

They will believe that you have all the time in the world to do what you want, and that you're rolling in the money. They'll think you can go on lavish vacations and that you don't have to answer to anyone. Take heart: The other business owners you meet will know the real story.

The secret to self-employed success

Passion. Without it you may be mildly successful, but you'll never be wildly successful!"

Find out more about Sheree's passion-driven business here—www.-fork-road.com. Listen to our interviews here http://www.cassandra-gaisford.com/media   and http://www.cassandragaisford.com/podcast/

I loved, loved, loved what Sheree shared and devoured every word —best of all there were no calories…so that was marvellous. What resonated with you?

Identify and record any lessons can you learn from Sheree's experience of discovering her calling and setting up her business which you could apply to starting your own business. Summarise some possible action steps.

WHAT YOU'VE LEARNED SO FAR

- Before committing yourself to starting your own business or being self-employed, you need to ask yourself whether you have what it takes
- Follow your heart, let your passion and intuition guide you towards the business you were born to create
- You have to believe in yourself—even when you don't
- You don't always need buckets of money, or the courage of a lion, to start your own business. You can start on a shoestring and feel the fear and begin anyway

- Starting a business doesn't have to be a full-time gig. You can start small and keep your current job while you watch your baby grow
- Caring about people and delivering something of value is the key to success

What's Next?

So, now you know the pitfalls of being self-employed and you know some of the joys. But do you really understand what YOU are looking for and why?

The next chapter will help you clarify the motivating forces driving your decisions. Knowing these will help boost your confidence when it comes to making an inspired leap.

WHY DO YOU WANT TO BE YOUR OWN BOSS?

**"*Wild horses wouldn't drag me back
to working for someone else.*"**
Alan Sugar, Entrepreneur and host of The Apprentice, UK

So now you know the pitfalls of being self-employed and you know some of the joys. But do you really understand what YOU are looking for and why?

Perhaps you can identify with Laura who wants to balance work commitments with caring for her young son. "My boss insists I go to the office. I can't understand why he won't let me work from home."

Do Your Own Thing

Creating your own business is one of the few ways you can generate an income doing what you want, when you want, with whom you want.

It can also be a great way to create an asset—one you can grow and sell later for a profit if you plan things right.

Employing yourself is also a great way to get a job when nobody else will hire you, or when you've lost your job. Like Wendy Pye, (her story is shared below), who started her own company and went from redundant to becoming a multi-millionaire.

Running your own business doesn't mean that you are going to be chained to your desk 24/ 7 as some people mistakenly believe. One of the important things prior to starting any new venture is to determine what you want to achieve and why.

ACTION TASK! Clarify what you really want

Write a list of benefits that self-employment will offer you. If you run out of ideas the following list may help. Identify how you want to feel, and what you want to have, and why this is important to you.

BENEFITS OF SELF Employment

Listed below are some of the benefits many people gain from being self-employed. Make a note of those most relevant to you and add these to the list you generated above.

Assess any options you are considering by creating a decision-making criteria checklist. For example, if time freedom is important for you, you may want to reconsider any plans to open a business where people expect you to be there at fixed hours.

- Time freedom—hours to suit yourself
- Flexibility
- No forced retirement age
- Autonomy
- Independence
- Making your own decisions
- Creativity
- Control
- Security–not worrying about corporate layoffs
- Live and work anywhere in the world
- Work from home
- Accountability
- Higher earnings
- Satisfaction and personal fulfilment
- Variety and freedom to be able to work on new ideas and create your own authentic style
- Combine diverse areas of interest, skill and enthusiasm
- Being guided by what feels right in your heart and intuition
- Freedom from financial stress
- Making a difference
- Freedom from the daily grind—a business that runs without you
- Being able to put all your passion and energy into

something you believe in, rather than something someone else believes in

- Creating an income producing asset

From Redundant to Multi-Millionaire

Necessity, as some say, is the mother of invention—and often it is the extra push many people need to take a leap into something new.

Some 55,000 New Zealanders are so-called 'necessity entrepreneurs,' people prompted by redundancy or unemployment to set up their own businesses, as distinct from 'opportunity entrepreneurs,' who've become self-employed as a result of planning and choice.

Wendy Pye is the mother of all necessity entrepreneurs. It took a good dose of adversity to get her entrepreneurial juices flowing and she hasn't looked back. She was dumped without warning from NZ News after 22 years with the company, given five minutes to clear her desk, and then marched off the premises.

With no job to go to Pye, then aged 42, set up her own educational publishing company. Now a multi-millionaire, she admits her motivation for going it alone was a desire to show her former employers what she could do.

"I was devastated and disappointed. But it really changed my life, which is a lot better now than if [redundancy] had never happened. I needed the push."

She certainly showed her former employers just what she could do. The 2015 National Business Review's Rich List, estimates Pye's personal wealth at $105 million.

She has fond thoughts for that executive who laid her off all those years ago. "That guy had vision," she says. "He knew something I didn't know. I can say that and laugh now."

Dubbed one of New Zealand's women power-brokers, Dame Wendy recently won the Business Entrepreneur category in the Women of Influence Awards.

The passion, determination and drive that helped her build her business into one of the most successful education export companies in the world shows no sign of slowing as she heads into her 70s.

Wendy Pye Publishing can now celebrate more than 2000 titles, in more than 20 countries, which have sold over 218 million copies. Her business has also developed digital learning platforms designed to teach children to read and write.

AGE IS **On Your Side**

Age is no barrier to employing yourself. Growing numbers of 40-plus men and women are taking up new challenges and starting businesses everyday. Being your own boss gives you more control over your future. If you love what you're doing, chances are you'll never want to retire.

Your life expectancy is on the rise. Which also means you'll be wanting enough money to live comfortably. Employing yourself will help you achieve that.

READY TO LEARN **some new tricks?**

As Brian Jones writes in his wonderful book, *Over 50? Start Your Business: Build Wealth, Control Your Destiny. Leave a Legacy*:

"Within the last twenty years, technologies such as functional magnetic response imaging (FMRI) have debunked the old-dog-new-tricks myth. Scientists have found that the brain can grow and make new connections at any age. The scientific term for this is neuroplasticity.

Now more than ever you can be, do and have nearly anything you desire. Like Annie, who aged 54, left teaching and became a romance writer.

COMPELLING EVIDENCE of Mid-Life Success

Loads of people have employed themselves or started their businesses in mid-life and beyond. Here's just a few:

- Joseph Campbell started Campbell's soup at age 52
- Arianna Huffington started the Huffington post at age 54
- Estee Lauder founded her cosmetics empire when she was 54
- Charles Flint started IBM at 61
- Amadeo Giannini founded the Bank of America when he was 60
- Col. Harlan Sanders launched KFC at age 65
- Heather Morris was 64 when she became a full-time author following her debut success with the publication of *The Tattooist of Auschwitz*

WILL YOU BE NEXT? What are you waiting for? If they can do it there's a strong likelihood you can too.

. . .

Action Task! Look For Your Heroes

Gather examples of mid-life entrepreneurs who inspire you. Allow them to be your virtual mentors. How can you use their success to guide and encourage you?

WHAT YOU'VE LEARNED SO FAR

- Intensify your desire, but keep it real. Get clear about what you want to gain by being your own boss and why
- Assess any options you are considering by creating a decision-making criteria checklist
- Sometimes life 'shouts' and gives you the push you need to start your business
- Courageous action can be inspired even at what seems the

worst of times. If life is dealing you a raw hand look for opportunities that may be disguised as setbacks

- Age is no barrier to self-employment

What's Next?

Now you have a clearer idea about both your 'what' and your 'why' is, and you have awakened your desire. The next step is to work out exactly what sort of business or self-employment opportunity is right for you.

To do this there is no better place to start than to determine what sets your heart on fire.

PURSUE YOUR PASSION NOT YOUR PENSION

"The starting point of all achievement is desire."
Napoleon Hill, Author

First things first! Start from the heart.

The first and most important commandment of choosing and growing your business is to follow your passion.

Creating a successful business that you'll love is impossible without passion, enthusiasm, zest, inspiration and the deep satisfaction that comes from doing something that delivers you some kind of buzz.

Passion is a source of energy from the soul, and when you combine it with a product or service that benefits others, that's where you'll find your magic.

Kevin Roberts, former CEO of global advertising agency Saatchi and Saatchi, passionately believes that love is the way forward for business.

Meeting peoples' needs, hopes, dreams, and desires, or offering something which helps them solve problems for which they'd love a cure, is good for people and it's good for business.

"For great brands to survive, they must create Loyalty Beyond Reason," he writes in his book *Lovemarks: The Future Beyond Brands*. Roberts argues, with a ton of facts, and emotionally evocative images to support his premise, that traditional branding practices have become stultified. What's needed are customer Love affairs. "The secret," he maintains, "is the use of Mystery, Sensuality, and Intimacy."

Other experts such as Simon Sinek, author of the bestselling book *Start With Why*, and Robert Kiyosaki entrepreneur and author of the *Rich Dad, Poor Dad* books, may urge you to begin with rational, head-based logic.

I'm advocating a similar, albeit less analytical approach to begin with. But the premise is similar, to create something meaningful for yourself, and for the customers and clients you wish to attract, you must believe in what you are doing. Your business idea must matter. You must know *why* it's important—to yourself and to others.

"'*Why*' is not money or profit—these are always the results. Why does your organisation exist? Why does it do the things it does? Why do customers really buy from one company or another?" challenges Sinek in his book.

I would add, *what* is its purpose? Roberts, would add, *how* can you make them fall in love with you and inspire loyalty beyond reason?

How to Find Your *Why*

When you discover and tap into your passion, you'll find your *why*. You'll also find a huge source of untapped potential that seems to be fearless and knows no bounds. Pursuing your passion in business is profitable on many levels.

Firstly, when you do what you love, this is most likely where your true talent lies, so you'll stand out in your field. Passion cannot be faked.

Secondly, you will be more enthusiastic about your pursuits. You will have more energy and tenacity to overcome obstacles, and more drive and determination to make things happen.

When you do what you care most about and believe in with such a passion, your work will be not something that you endure, but something that you enjoy. More importantly, work will become a vehicle for self-expression.

Thirdly, passion attracts. As multi-millionaire businesswoman Anita Roddick once said, '*We communicate with passion and passion sells.*'

Ms Roddick founded her company, The Body Shop, on one simple premise—beauty products tested on animals was cruel, barbaric, unnecessary and immoral. Millions of men and women around the world agreed.

People like to do business with people who are passionate about their products and services. When global financial services company KPMG re-branded with passion as a core theme, profitability soared. Check out my presentation on Slideshare to find out how:

http://www.slideshare.net/CassandraGaisford/passionslides-with-kpmg-slides

HEARTS ON FIRE

The key to sound business planning begins from the inside out. First you need to determine who you are, who you want to be, and what you want to contribute to the world. In working this out, there is no better place to start than with finding out what sets you heart on fire and *why*.

Michael Jr. Comedy, a stand-up comedian and author, explains how discovering your *why* helps you develop options that enable you to live and work with purpose.

"When you know your *why*, you have options on what your *what* can be. For instance, my *why* is to inspire people to walk in purpose. My *what* is stand-up comedy. My *what* is writing books.... Another *what* that has moved me toward my *why* is a web series that we have out now called Break Time."

Check out this clip from one of Michael's most successful episodes http://bit.ly/1PnOTrH. You'll see how working with passion and purpose awakens dormant talents and enables souls to fly higher.

"When you know your *why* your *what* has more impact because you are walking toward your purpose," says Michael.

. . .

WE'LL DIVE DEEPER into discovering your life purpose in the following chapter.

SURF the Web

http://www.eofire.com: Fuel your inspiration by checking out this top-ranked business Podcast where some of the most inspiring entrepreneurs are interviewed 7-days a week. Founder and host John Lee Dumas shares his journey from frustrated employee to inspired entrepreneur via video here http://www.eofire.com/about/

DISCOVERING Your Passion

Everyone is capable of passion; some people just need help taking it out of the drawer. Look for the clues. Often this involves noticing the times you feel most energised and alive, or when you experience a surge of adrenaline through your body.

Sometimes it's the moments when time seems to fly. Perhaps it is something you love to do and would willingly do for free.

Passion is not always about love. The things that push your buttons can lead you to the things that you're most passionate about.

Working long hours, too much stress, financial strain or a whole raft of other constant pressures can soon send you drowning in a sea of negativity—killing your passion and robbing you of the energy and positivity you need to make a life-enhancing change.

If stress is taking a toll on your life you may want to check out the first book in the *Mid-Life Career Rescue* series, *The Call For Change*.

The strategies and tips in the book will help you restore the balance and get your mojo back. You'll also learn how to boost your ability to generate ideas to get unstuck. Available on in paperback and eBook will help.

If you need more help to you manage stress my book, *Stress Less. Love Life More: How to Stop Worrying, Reduce Anxiety, Eliminate Negative Thinking and Find Happiness*, available as a paperback and eBook from all good online book stores will help.

ACTION TASK! Find Your Passion

Real passion is more than a fad or a fleeting enthusiasm. It can't be turned on and off like a light switch. Answering the following questions will help you begin to clarify the things you are most passionate about:

1. **When does time seem to fly?** When was the last time you felt really excited, or deeply absorbed in, or obsessed by something? What were you doing? Who were you with? What clues did you notice?
2. **What do you care deeply or strongly about?** Discovering all the things that you believe in is not always easy. Look for the clues to your deep beliefs by catching the times you use words such as 'should' or 'must.'
3. **What do you value?** What do you need to experience, feel, or be doing to feel deeply fulfilled?
4. **What pushes your buttons or makes you angry?** How could you use your anger constructively to bring about change?
5. **Which skills and talents come most easily or naturally to you?** Which skills do you love using? What skills do you look forward to using? What gives you such a buzz or a huge sense of personal satisfaction that you'd keep doing it even if you weren't paid?

6. **What inspires you?** To be inspired is to be in spirit. What bewitches and enthrals you so much that you lose all track of time? What makes your soul sing? What floats your boat? What things, situations, people, events etc. fill you with feelings of inspiration? List all your obsessions and the things that interest you deeply. If you're struggling to identify your interests and inspirations, you'll find some handy prompts in the next chapter.

7. **Keep a passion journal.** My passion is passion—to help others live and work with passion and to bring about positive change in the world. If you're not sure what you are passionate about, creating a passion journal is one simple but powerful technique to help achieve clarity. Your passion journal is where manifesting your preferred future really happens. I've been keeping a passion journal for years and so many things I've visualised and affirmed on the pages, are now my living realities—personally and professionally.

Love Is Where The Magic Is

Love is where the magic is. When you love what you do with such a passion you'd do it for free this is your path with heart. You've heard the saying, 'when you do what you love, you'll never work again.' It's true. Work doesn't feel like a slog, it feels energising.

As Annie Featherston, writing as Sophia James, shared in the second book on the *Mid-Life Career Rescue* series, *What Makes You Happy*, "When you combine your favourite skills with doing something you completely and utterly love, you come home to your True Self and find your place of bliss. The result? Contentment—and more often than not, producing something highly marketable."

. . .

Passion in Business

A good way to find your own passion and identify ways to turn it into a fulfilling self-employment opportunity is to look for examples of others who have started businesses they are passionate about.

Here are just a few of many examples:

A passion for bugs! Brian Clifford is passionate about helping people and bugs. He has combined his passion into a successful business as a pest controller.

"All the rats, all the maggots, all the cockroaches all over the place, these are the things that I love doing,' he says. His business motto is, 'If it bugs you, I'll kill it!"

Check out his business here >> www.borercontrolwellington.co.nz

A passion for bones! John Holley has turned his passion for bones into a business, Skulls Down Under, selling skeletons to museums all over the world.

Check out his business here >> www.skullsdownunder.co.nz

A passion for Maori food. Charles Royal's passion for finding a way to incorporate traditional Maori foods into modern dishes led him to start his own business—Kinaki Wild Herbs.

"I had learned a lot about the bush during my time in the army and have taken that knowledge through the years, developing food tours and cooking classes using what we gather from the wild. I love organics and making something out of nothing, but you have to know what you are looking for," says Royal. Air New Zealand now serves pikopiko and horopito in its First and Business Classes.

Check out his business here >> www.maorifood.com

SUCCESS STORY: A LOVE OF GOOD FOOD

"Passion is Everything—If You Don't Have It You Will Not Succeed"

A love of good food and a lifelong dream to open their passion-driven business in London fuelled Wellington restauranteurs Vivienne Haymans and Ashley Sumners' move to the UK.

"We both felt we had gone as far as we could with our business in New Zealand and wanted to move further afield," says Vivienne.

"I came here for a three-month holiday, secretly wanting to stay longer and build a business overseas. On arriving I discovered that London seriously needed a restaurant like our Sugar Club in Wellington. There was nowhere in London doing anything like it. I called Ash and a year later he also moved to London after selling our Wellington restaurant."

They relocated the restaurant to Notting Hill in 1995, then to Soho in 1998, winning the Time Out "Best Modern British Restaurant" award in 1996 and "Best Central London

Restaurant" award in 1999, along with several Evening Standard Eros awards.

Since then they have expanded and diversified their restaurant business, opening a chain of modern *traiteurs* (Italian-style delicatessens) that offer delicious, easy-to-prepare hand-made meals and great New Zealand coffee.

The first of these is called The Grocer on Elgin, situated in the heart of Notting Hill. Vivienne designed all three restaurants and 'The Grocer On' stores.

Like many people following their passion, Vivienne and Ash faced significant barriers before finally making it big.

"It took Ash and I seven years to fulfil our dream of opening The Sugar Club in London. When we first arrived there were huge premiums being asked for restaurant sites.

Then, with the early 90s recession they were giving restaurants away but, like now, the banks were not lending. We had no property assets at the time, limited funds, a reference from our NZ lawyer, accountant and bank manager and a handful of NZ press clippings. The banks wanted property assets and UK business records. No less."

Just when it looked like the obstacles were insurmountable, their passion for great food and design, the quality of the produce, and the integrity of its production, produced lucky fruit.

"We were offered a site by a landlord that we had had dealings with in the past. He liked what we did and gave us the lease. We developed the old Singapore Pandang into the Notting Hill Sugar Club. I borrowed an extra £5000 from my mum and paid her back in a month. It was an instant success and well worth the long wait."

Vivienne says that following their passion is an important ingredient in their success.

"Passion is everything—if you don't have it you will not succeed. It is hard work; your passion will pull you through the seriously bad times, which will always occur."

Hot Tip! Gathering your own examples of passionate people and businesses is a great way to build confidence and generate your own business ideas.

HERE ARE some things that other people who are self-employed are passionate about:

- **Creating Businesses**—Entrepreneurs Melissa Clarke Reynolds and Eric Watson
- **Airports**—Graham is an airport designer
- **Boats**—Bill Day runs a specialist maritime service business
- **Beauty**—Joy Gaisford, Designer
- **Food**—Ruth Pretty, Caterer and food writer
- **Astronomy**—Richard Hall, Stonehenge Aotearoa
- **Design**—Luke Pierson, runs a web design business
- **Rocks**—Carl created Carlucciland—a rock-themed amusement park
- **Passion**—Cassandra Gaisford helping people work and live their passion!

HERE ARE some things that some businesses are passionate about:

- **Animal Welfare and Human Rights**—The Body Shop
- **Technology**—Microsoft, Apple
- **Helping people**—Worklife Solutions, Venus Network
- **Equality**—The EEO Trust, and the Johnstone Group
- **The Environment**—The Conservation Department
- **Honey**—The Honey Hive
- **Chocolate**—Chocaholic
- **Pampering Others**—East Day Spa

TUNE In To Your Body Barometer

What pushes your buttons or makes you angry? Having my manager threaten to 'smash my head in,' and working with others who were bullies and tyrants, the relentless pursuit of profit at the expense of caring for people, and numerous work restructurings, motivated me to gain my independence.

That and getting shingles—something I wrote about in my first books, *The Call for Change*, and also *What Makes You Happy*.

Shingles was definitely my body barometer sending me a red alert! As was seeing my colleagues suffer heart attacks.

As Neale Walsch, the author of *Conversations with God*, says, "Judge not about which you feel passionate. Simply notice it, then see if it serves you, given who and what you wish to be."

So, as I've mentioned earlier, rather than become bitter, I thought how could I use my anger constructively to bring about change?

I decided I wanted to help people find jobs that made them happy, and I wanted to help victims of workplace bullying. That was my *why* and my *what*.

Stepping Stones to Success

I started a career counselling business for an established workplace counselling organisation before going out on my own.

Working as an employee first gave me the confidence to fly free. I became more motivated when the CEO changed and the new boss tried to manage me. Increasingly, the job began to frustrate me.

It lacked challenge, my salary was capped, and I was finding it increasingly difficult to balance childcare. The final clincher however was when I did the math.

I worked out my hourly rate as a full-time salaried employee, versus what they charged me out per hour, and how much business I was bringing in for them, and came to the conclusion they were buying my skills, but they weren't paying me enough. I could work less and earn and achieve more if I employed myself. I started to feel excited!

Action Task! Tune into Your Body Barometer

Notice the times you feel strong emotions. These could be annoyance, irritation and anger. Or they could be a sense of excitement, a state of arousal, a feeling of limitless energy, a burning desire, a strong gut feeling, a feeling of contentment or determination. Notice these feelings and record them in your passion journal.

Go deeper. Ask, "How could I make a living from my passion?" or "How do others make a living from things that excite or motivate me?"

Explore possibilities. Even a simple Google search, or generating ideas with others could get you started down the right path.

** FREE BONUS **

If you haven't downloaded the free copy of the Passion Workbook, download it <u>here</u> >>https://dl. bookfunnel.com/aepj97k2n1

WHAT YOU'VE LEARNED SO FAR

- Passion is energy. It is emotion, zest, intensity, enthusiasm and excitement. Passion is love
- Creating more love in the world is the way forward for business. Meeting peoples' needs, hopes, dreams and desires, or offering something which helps them solve problems for which they'd love a cure, is good for people and its good for business
- Do what moves you. Pursuing your passion, not your

pension, can be a liberating and clarifying catalyst to your true calling and the business you were born to create

- A healthy obsession can lead to many things. Not only will your passion lead you to your path with heart, it will also help fuel the fires of determination, courage and self-belief. You'll be fully alive, stand out from the crowd and gain a competitive edge

- If you don't know where to look, passion can be difficult to find. Tune into your body barometer and notice the times when you feel most alive, inspired or fulfilled

- Start a passion journal—keep track of the times when you notice clues to your passion, such as a feeling of inspiration or any of the other signs discussed in this chapter. Record these moments so that they don't get lost or forgotten

- Adding quotes, pictures or any other insights will really make your journal come alive. Gain greater awareness of what drives your passion by asking yourself, "Why am I passionate about this?" Look for the themes and patterns that build up over time

- Keep your passion alive by updating your journal and referring to it regularly. Actively look for examples of people who have made the things you are passionate about into a rewarding business

What's Next?

In the next chapter you'll discover how joyous and exciting work and life is when you're working with a higher purpose.

DID YOU ENJOY THIS EXCERPT?

If you need more help and a step-by-step guide to becoming your own boss my book, *Employ Yourself,* available as a paperback and eBook from all good online bookstores will help.

To fuel the flames of inspiration to help you create a passion and purpose inspired business, The Passion-Driven Business Planning Journal:The Effortless Path to Manifesting Your Business and Career Goals, available as a paperback and ebook from all good online bookstores will help.

Or you may prefer to take my online course, and watch inspirational and practical videos and other strategies to help you to fulfil your potential—https://the-coaching-lab.teachable.com/p/follow-your-passion-and-purpose-to-prosperity.